IMAGINING A CHURCH IN THE SPIRIT

IMAGINING A CHURCH IN THE SPIRIT

A Task for
Mainline Congregations

BEN CAMPBELL JOHNSON *and* GLENN McDONALD

WILLIAM B. EERDMANS PUBLISHING COMPANY
GRAND RAPIDS, MICHIGAN / CAMBRIDGE, U.K.

© 1999 Wm. B. Eerdmans Publishing Co.
255 Jefferson Ave. S.E., Grand Rapids, Michigan 49503 /
P.O. Box 163, Cambridge CB3 9PU U.K.

Printed in the United States of America

04 03 02 01 00 99   7 6 5 4 3 2 1

Library of Congress Cataloging-in-Publication Data

Johnson, Ben Campbell.
Imagining a church in the spirit: a task for mainline congregations /
Ben C. Johnson and Glenn McDonald.
p.   cm.
ISBN 0-8028-4663-7 (pbk.)
1. Church renewal.   I. McDonald, Glenn.   II. Title.
BV600.2.J55   1999
262'.001'7 — dc21   99-31079
CIP

Contents

97559

Why and How to Use this Book

LEADERS IN THE CHURCH today are caught in a crisis, a moment of threat and opportunity. Unless mainline congregations imagine anew what it means to be "church," they will face even further decline and irrelevance. Yet, these very congregations in need of change continue to offer strong resistance to the shifts that lead to the necessary transformations.

Imagining the church in new forms with alternative practices, a professor and a practitioner joined efforts to provide help for the task. Ben Johnson, professor of Christian Spirituality at Columbia Theological Seminary, and Glenn McDonald, pastor of the Zionsville Presbyterian Church in Zionsville, Indiana, lay out the theological foundation and share practical strategies for imagining a Church in the Spirit. One brings years of working at the task of church renewal and twenty years as a professor; the other offers a dozen years of experience in beginning and pastoring a new church. The professor provides the conceptual text and the pastor a corroborative witness.

Professor Johnson has written about the new cultural context and its impact on mainline congregations. His ideas in *New Day/New Church* and *95 Theses for the Church* provide the backdrop for this task of reimagining mainline congregations.

The conviction that new church developments and traditional congregations must face the task of imagining their life and ministry in new and effective ways compels a fresh, workable approach to the necessary changes. Jesus Christ, risen and living and our present Lord, provides the key to rethinking the church. To illustrate how this core conviction might work, the authors have chosen crucial aspects of the church — community, initiation, prayer, mission, preaching, inclusivity, leadership, and teaching — as the focus of their efforts. They have offered practical and theologically sound ways these tasks can be addressed by congregations.

This text was written for both lay and clergy. Students, whether taking their first degree or an advanced degree, will find this book instructive. Pastors will find these ideas stimulating for their preaching and teaching. This text will also serve church officials well; perhaps they could read and discuss a chapter before each monthly meeting. Sunday school classes will find the questions for discussion thought-provoking, and individual lay members will find them a guide to their reflection. The material in this book can provide the substance for an officers' retreat. In all these situations this material will serve as a resource for introducing constructive change in congregations of all sizes.

Many deserve thanks for making this book possible. Professor Johnson thanks George Telford, Director of Advanced Studies at Columbia Seminary, for inviting him to teach doctoral students in a summer session. The basic outline of the book came in response to that opportunity. He also expresses thanks to his wife, Nan, for typing changes in the manuscript. Pastor McDonald extends his gratitude to the Zionsville Church for sharing with him in these discoveries and for a four-month sabbatical that gave him time to write. Also, appreciation to Mary Sue, his wife, who graciously gave up time with him so he could finish the project.

These writers hope that congregations of all sizes and forms will respond eagerly to the opportunity before us. Both imagine that pastors, officials, and leaders in congregations will engage these ideas seriously, pray for guidance for the church, open themselves to the fresh and powerful winds of the Spirit, and permit themselves to imagine the church as it can be in the twenty-first century.

CHAPTER ONE

A New Church Vision

MAINLINE CHURCHES in North America are in trouble. This is no new insight; they have been in trouble for three decades. Membership is declining, money from the constituency is shrinking, and most denominations are downsizing. As a consequence of the decline in numbers, the mainline denominations have been enticed by the church growth movement as a means of replacing members. Decline is a problem, but it is not the real problem.

In the last three decades these denominations have become captive to social issues, shifting from one injustice to another. First, it was the role of women, then the place of ethnic groups and minorities. On the heels of these challenges came the abortion issue, and then the ordination of gays and lesbians. The focus has shifted according to the strength of the issue and the advocates it mobilized. Each of these struggles succeeded in depositing in the church special interest groups who seek to keep the issue alive until it is favorably resolved. The shifting focus from one issue to another presents a problem in ministry, but this is not the greatest problem facing mainline congregations.

Church leadership has been whimsical about its particular role in the revitalizing of congregations and in making a social witness. The changing image of the minister has contributed to this tentativeness. A few decades ago the minister was dubbed the "Pastoral Director"; administering the program of the congregation became the minister's controlling preoccupation. The therapist model followed closely, a model in which the pastor served as the healer through counseling and preaching. The social service of the church followed the therapeutic, and response to human pain — especially pain on the margins of the church — dominated its vision for ministry. In recent years the minister as CEO, Chief Executive Officer, has taken center stage, and the church has adopted a management model without serious criticism of its limitations. Identity confusion and alternating styles of leadership have created problems for the church, but even these are not the most crucial problems in mainline congregations.

Although my allusion to the church growth movement does not imply disfavor with evangelism and enlarging the congregation, getting more members is not the major crisis in mainline churches. To suggest that mainline churches are issue-driven does not mean issues are unimportant, but it does raise the question of whether resolving issues is the central mission of the church. Pointing to the shifting role of pastors and leaders of congregations does not intend to deprecate pastors, but to hint at the loss of vision and thus the loss of a clear identity. We face a greater problem than any of these concerns.

The greatest problem facing mainline congregations in North America is the loss of vision. We have been blinded to the living Christ among us.

This blindness keeps the church from seeing itself as "the body of Christ" and Christ alive in his body continuing his mission through it today. Our greatest need is a vision of his living presence, here and now working through the members of the body. If we possessed a vision of Christ as the foundation of the church, the life of the church and the Lord of the church, and if we could reimagine all the functions of the church as the corporate expression of Christ, we would be on a high road to recovery.

The consequence of losing the sense of Christ's presence in and among us here and now has changed the vital fellowship of believers into an institution; and the institution, rather than radiating the presence of the Spirit, often shields us from it. Forgetting the presence among us has produced lifeless gatherings of the baptized with neither vision nor passion for their mission. Perhaps delineating a few characteristics of these congregations which I call "Old Church," the church of another generation, will make the point clearer.

The Character of Old Church

Our observation of mainline congregations suggests that many, if not most, are going through the motions of being a church but without spiritually transformative power and spiritual urgency. These congregations may be characterized as:

- Keeping alive the memory of Christ and his teachings.
- Offering a form of worship designed mostly for a pre-1950s generation.
- Functioning to legitimate the social, economic, and political practices of the culture.
- Fulfilling societal needs like caring for hurting members, marrying, burying, and baptizing.
- Possessing members who are morally good, productive citizens who want their lives to count for something beyond themselves.
- Encouraging persons to become generous givers in comparison with persons in every other culture in the world.

In addition to these more positive characteristics, most of these congregations

- are homogeneous with the membership very much alike in education, income, social values, and habits, with no evidence of the inclusivity of the body of Christ.
- possess a superficial grasp of the Christian faith, knowing the creed, some prayers, and a few hymns.
- lack the practice of prayer, scripture study, and ministry.
- downplay theology as being for ministers and a few elite lay persons.
- do not speak of their Christian faith with each other and are too embarrassed to speak about it with persons outside the church.

3

- believe in God but do not experience, nor do they expect to experience, the presence of God in a personal, ongoing manner.
- adopt lifestyles and values that fit comfortably into the dominant culture, with no conflict between their views and those of persons outside the church.
- offer a place to build social relationships that meet their own social needs without much thought of the needs of others.
- demonstrate a strong interest in self-preservation.
- seek persons to serve the church's ends.
- lack clarity about their essential mission in the world.
- are composed of marginally active members, with 20 percent of the membership doing 80 percent of the work and giving most of the money.

Can this church embark on its mission to serve the world and proclaim the gospel of Christ to all nations without a profound transformation of life and vision? Does not this church need a vision of itself as the body of Christ, a community in which he lives and acts?

Toward the Recovery of Vision

Our problem today is not unique; in fact, it is about as old as the church itself. In the first century, the second generation of Christians had grown weary and lost the original vision. Their parents had expected the return of Jesus in their lifetime. Certainly, he would return in the next generation's lifetime, and when he did not, they became discouraged and their passion for mission cooled. Luke, in his Gospel and the Acts of the Apostles, sought to help them see that the Jesus who had been among their parents in the flesh had indeed returned in the Spirit. Pentecost marked his dramatic return when he was incarnated in the waiting disciples in the upper room. And, Luke argued, this presence among them was even better than his being with the apostles in the flesh. Now, in the Spirit, Christ could be with all persons, everywhere, all the time. Luke offered these hapless Christians a new vision of their situation, a vision that would eventually change their lives, deepen their fellowship, and inspire their engagement in mission.

We must address the same task as Luke, the Gospel writer, who helped discouraged believers get a new vision of the presence of our risen, living Lord. Perhaps our disillusionment does not originate in the failed return of Jesus but in the ineffectiveness of our congregations to give a powerful, life-changing witness to the gospel, or their failure to make much of an impression on the emerging culture. Without question, North American Christians live in a new day created by the explosion of communication, global mobility, the breakdown of old certainties inherited from the Enlightenment, and the birth of a generation completely ignorant of its Christian roots — to name just a few of its driving forces. And, the old ways of being and doing church do not work in this radically changing culture. We need a new vision of the church and fresh ways of fulfilling our calling.

In Search of a Vision

What do we mean by vision? The capacity to see, to picture the future church in a manner that evokes a compelling urgency; in this instance, to grasp what the church must become in the century that lies before us. The compelling image of this future church will result from a daring act of imagination that creates a picture of what Christ calls his body to be and do. The old cultural model has broken down, and the new church vision has not formed; we are living between the times, a time of revisioning. This vision of the church for which we search must grasp the essential aspects of the church — initiation, prayer, teaching, healing, community, preaching, and worship — and reimagine them in a new situation. To confront this crisis, the church needs visionaries who recreate with integrity forms of the church's life which are both faithful and relevant. The core question of today's visionaries is: "What will a faithful church look like in the twenty-first century?" This challenge to revision the church presents us with a life-or-death option.

Missionaries to other cultures have always engaged in this creative translation of the gospel into new and different contexts. Are we not missionaries in an alien culture faced with the task of doing the creative, imaginative missionary work of translation?

This task will compel us to focus on the essence of the church, that which makes the church the church, the non-negotiable aspects of the church. The community of Christ must re-present Christ, his person and his mission, in an authentic form. How do we imagine this new form of the church for ministry today? Old structures have already proved inadequate; new ones have yet to be born. Also, we struggle with systems that have become irrelevant to Western, secular people, and lack the power to transform life. Increasingly, these old religious practices are like straitjackets restraining the mission of Christ. A compelling vision will break through these restraints and liberate the church to fulfill its mission.

Without a compelling vision, a church lacks direction, movement, a way of orderly transition and cohesiveness. A clear vision helps the congregation at just these points. For example, a vision creates a sense of direction for the church. Without a vision, the ministry of a congregation tends to sit on dead center. A self-centered community looks inward and repeats programs that have become sacred to the congregation. Vision works against these stifling practices and breaks the status quo. The vision serves the congregation like the North Star serves the explorer. When the congregation comes to a turning point, the vision, like the star, gives a sense of direction.

A vision initiates movement. Unlike writing objective mission statements, a vision involves passion, a deep emotional commitment to the new possibility. Vision energizes the congregation. A compelling vision will challenge the church's modes of worship and practices of ministry; vision draws the congregation toward a new future. A new way of seeing the future gives courage to experiment with new forms of worship or a fresh approach to decision making. When these changes occur, they give the congregation courage to move toward its dreams. Through these movements a congregation will begin to change, and each small change provides greater motivation and strength to be conformed to Christ. The vision, like a magnet, draws the congregation into the future.

Yet, a vision does more than point the church in a new direction and initiate movement; it also provides a dialectic within which "the Church in the Spirit" may be negotiated. The picture of future church creates a contrast between the actual and the possible, and defines a free space for the continuous interplay between "what is" and "what is becoming." When leaders in a congregation propose a different future, inevitably they face resistance. Those committed to present ways of doing and being church will catalogue all the reasons why the church should remain as it is, but those possessed with a vision will continue to speak about what might be in the future. This dialogue between what is and what is to be provides a constructive way of change. The dialogue serves change dynamically by forcing the church forward, then backward, then forward in incremental steps.

Finally, the vision offers cohesion during the change process. The vision, like glue, holds together the actual and the possible; without this adhesive the church will tend to pull apart. When leaders stop talking with each other, lose respect for each other, or when they fight for control of the situation more than they seek the will of God, the congregation splits. Thus, it is imperative to keep the dialectic alive by continuing to negotiate the vision. Remember! It is never God's will to split the church. To maintain unity, we must keep the conversation open, listen to all the voices at the table, and keep refining the vision until all have a place in the church of the future.

Perhaps an illustration will clarify what the vision achieves in a changing congregation. Suppose a church that has suffered for years with introversion, self-preoccupation, and loss of vision for its mission calls new leadership. A new pastor arrives on the scene with a sense of being called by Christ to serve the people of God. After the new pastor comes, things begin to happen: attendance picks up, interest heightens, new ministries begin.

All this takes place because the new pastor believes she serves with Christ through his body, in which Christ is present in individual members and in the gathered community. As she goes about her pastoral tasks, she looks for signs of Christ in the members as well as in persons outside the church. She discerns the latent vision in these persons. A fragment of a vision of Christ, living in and ministering through this body, begins to form in her soul. She discusses it with the leaders in the church, and she speaks of the vision with marginal members and even those outside the congregation. As she talks and listens, the vision becomes more definite and her conversations plant the seed of vision in all she meets.

The vision that resides in the pastor finds its way into sermons that challenge the congregation and deepen their understanding of their mission. Worship, administration, and pastoral care begin to be shaped by the vision. The vision presents a constant challenge to both the leaders and the members. Under the impact of a new picture of the future, the congregation begins to serve the needs of persons in their neighborhood; the vision will not let them sit with complacency on the sidelines. The vision pulls the church forward while some members resist and others try to assimilate the challenge. These groups struggle with each other, yet the vision keeps tension on the church to move forward. And, as this church lives into a vision, that vision has the power to hold dissident groups together while changes are negotiated.

The Church's Vision: Jesus Christ the Foundation

To conceive a vision of the Church in the Spirit, we must begin with Jesus Christ. The faithful church in every age must be grounded in the person, ministry, and teaching of Jesus Christ. The church is his body, the earthly form of his existence; he is the cornerstone of the church. The reimagined Church in the Spirit requires Jesus Christ as its foundation. Saint Paul wrote to the Corinthian church:

> According to the grace of God given to me, like a skilled master builder I laid a foundation, and someone else is building on it. Each builder must choose with care how to build on it. For no one can lay any foundation other than the one that has been laid; that foundation is Jesus Christ. Now if anyone builds on the foundation with gold, silver, precious stones, wood, hay, straw — the work of each builder will become visible, for the Day will disclose it, because it will be revealed with fire, and the fire will test what sort of work

8

each has done. If what has been built on the foundation survives, the builder will receive a reward. If the work is burned up, the builder will suffer loss; the builder will be saved, but only as through fire. (1 Cor. 3:10-15)

We take Paul's statement at face value: "For no one can lay any foundation other than the one that has been laid; that foundation is Jesus Christ." This foundation includes his birth, life, death, resurrection, and living presence.

Christ is the divine presence that permeates the church. Weekly we confess our belief in his death and resurrection, and we rehearse these core convictions when we break bread and drink wine together. The Eucharist celebrates his presence at the Table, but do we actually experience the presence? Too often we have become blind to the presence and have continued running the church on a memory rather than actual communion with the living Lord.

Yet, the promise of presence seems so clear in Christ's closing talks with his disciples. In the Upper Room discourse he said, "I will not leave you orphaned; I am coming to you. In a little while the world will no longer see me, but you will see me; because I live, you also will live. On that day you will know that I am in my Father, and you in me, and I in you" (John 14:18-20). In this amazing promise Jesus makes it clear that after his death he will return to his followers. He will give them life, not merely physical life but his life, the life of God, and in addition to that life, an assurance of their being in union with him, with each other, and with the Father.

As presence in us and in our midst, Christ promises to keep revealing himself to his followers, not only to the apostles, but also to all those who believe in him. This promised presence will teach you all things, bring to your remembrance what he has said, speak what he hears, show you things to come, and lead you into all truth (John 16:12-15). What Jesus began in the flesh, he continues in the Spirit through his corporate body. The church derives its nature from Christ. He was Son of God and Son of Mary, that is, he was both truly human and truly divine in an inseparable manner. The church will always be a human community that is permeated by the Spirit of the risen Christ;

it will therefore be human with all the problems associated with fallen humanity and at the same time be a bearer of the holy.

This paradigmatic Christ also shapes the church by what he did. A cursory reading of the Gospels depicts his ministry: he healed the sick, fed the hungry, showed compassion to the oppressed; he questioned the tradition of the elders, confronted religious and political authorities with penetrating insight; he suffered faithfully for the truth and triumphed by the will and power of God.

Every action of Jesus provides material for reflection and meditation on the nature and mission of the church. What he did in the flesh, he continues to do through our flesh, his body on earth. Our cues for ministry come from him and his actions.

Jesus provides a paradigm for the church's nature and mission in what he taught and how he taught. As a teacher he proclaimed a kingdom that embraces the whole of creation and manifests itself in human history as preserver of meaning, creator of justice, and force for liberation. This kingdom breaks into history at unannounced moments and mysteriously transforms it.

He taught about God as compassionate and forgiving, and emphasized the primacy of absolute faith in the Father, the Creator of the Universe and the Author of History. This faith leads to a worry-free life because the One who cares for the lilies and the birds also cares about human beings. His teaching gives priority to the spiritual aspects of life because life is much more than meeting physical necessities. Jesus both taught and demonstrated the goodness of God to all persons in all circumstances. He emphasized that to realize yourself you must deny yourself. Jesus taught that humans have value not only to themselves but also to God.

If we understand Jesus as a paradigm for the church's being and mission, his incarnation defines the church as a divine-human community. His ministry sets forth our mission as one of witness, compassion, and justice. His teaching provides both the content of Christian faith and a model for teaching others. These foundational convictions will provide the basis for our reimagining the church as the body of Christ in the Spirit.

The Metaphors of the Church

The writers of the New Testament captured the dynamic life of the church in a variety of metaphors. These metaphors point to the unutterable reality of the intimate relation of the holy presence to a human community. Each metaphor underscores the urgency of recapturing a vision of the church in its intimate relation to Christ's living presence.

The temple signifies the dwelling place of God on earth. It contained holy things like the Ark of the Covenant and the Holy of Holies. It was a place to which the people came to transact with God. The church, not as building but as community, is the temple of the living God. The community of baptized believers forms the dwelling place of the Spirit. "Do you not know," asks the apostle Paul, "that you are God's temple and that God's Spirit dwells in you? If anyone destroys God's temple, God will destroy that person. For God's temple is holy, and you are that temple" (1 Cor. 3:16-17).

St. Peter spoke of this phenomenon as the people of God. "Once you were not a people, but now you are God's people; once you had not received mercy, but now you have received mercy" (1 Peter 2:10). This metaphor emphasizes family, the family of God. God is the progenitor, Christ the Elder Brother, and the Spirit is the Mother who gives birth to new life in the community. This people draws life from God and creates a new social milieu expressive of the intention and purpose of God in the world.

St. John speaks of the relation of Christ to the members of the church as a vine with its branches. This metaphor suggests that the life of Christ flows into the community like sap from the vine flows into the branches. He is the life, the source of fruit and growth; without him the branches wither, die, and are cast off. St. John records Jesus' admonition to his disciples: "Abide in me as I abide in you. Just as the branch cannot bear fruit by itself unless it abides in the vine, neither can you unless you abide in me. I am the vine, you are the branches. Those who abide in me and I in them bear much fruit, because apart from me you can do nothing" (John 15:4-6).

St. Paul calls the church the body of Christ. "Now you are the body of Christ and individually members of it" (1 Cor. 12:27). This metaphor speaks of Christ's community and of its mission. The church is Christ's "earthly form of existence." The church re-presents Christ in communal form. Together we constitute his body, and as such he continues to do through us what he did on earth.

The writer of the letter to the Ephesians speaks of the church as the bride of Christ. This metaphor graphically depicts our intimacy with Christ; he is as intimate with the church as a husband with his bride. Christ is as intimately joined to his body as a man is to a woman in commitment, love, and sexual intercourse! This closeness of Christ encompasses each individual and the whole community. The Ephesians author says, "Husbands, love your wives, just as Christ loved the church and gave himself up for her, in order to make her holy by cleansing her with the washing of water by the word, so as to present the church to himself in splendor, without a spot or wrinkle or anything of the kind — yes, so that she may be holy and without blemish" (Eph. 5:25-27).

Each of these metaphors clearly speaks of the church with a peculiar emphasis on the presence of God in this community. Our supreme need in making the transition into the future is a vision of the church as an embodiment of the presence of Christ and a bearer of the sacred.

The Church in the Spirit

All that has been affirmed through the church about the person of Christ, the teaching of Christ, and the mission of Christ, has profound significance in helping us recognize Christ's presence with us and his life in his body today. The church need not live on a memory of a memory or a second-hand report; it can live in the spirit of prophecy, in the presence and power of the contemporaneous Christ.

The Church in the Spirit lives with the awareness of the indwelling Christ; he is with us, in us, and wills to empower and guide us. Yet, this is not new. He has always guided and empowered the church when it has been willing to listen and obey. The Church in the Spirit is a community of the Real Presence, the embodiment of the risen and living Lord, the community infused with transcendence, and the witness to the coming kingdom.

Our day requires that we identify the essential aspects of the church, the facets of the church that are Christ, that manifest his person, ministry, and his teaching through these formative images, and through the power of the Spirit we can imagine the church as a re-presentation of Christ in today's culture. Surely a Church in the Spirit must be

- a living community of faith composed of living stones that draw their life from the foundation stone.
- an incarnate community formed in a particular cultural setting through which the living presence of its Lord manifests himself in the faith, values, relationships, service, and outreach of his community.
- a worshiping community that gathers to offer praise and thanksgiving to the Creator, to implore God's help, and to rehearse regularly its identity and calling.
- a transformative community through the presence of the living Lord, so that all who enter into the community encounter him, and through their encounter in worship, service, and reflection they are made whole and empowered for ministry.
- an inclusive community that embraces differences — rich and poor, male and female, powerful and weak — because Christ has reconciled all persons to God.
- a unified community through the Spirit, in which all who enter have drunk of the Spirit of Christ and are joined to each other in baptism.
- a missional community that is being sent into the world to serve.

Can we imagine this church?

A Corroborative Witness

Our thirteen-year-old son Mark had never issued a complaint about his eyesight. Nothing would have prompted us to schedule an eye exam except the recurrent gentle suggestion of our pediatrician: "You really ought to do that sometime, just to be sure." Thus we were more than a little surprised when Mark's appointment resulted in a prescription for eyeglasses. "Note how his eyes aren't quite on the same level," said the examiner. "I'm going to recommend prism lenses."

I had never heard of prism lenses. When they arrived two weeks later the family gathered for a trying-on party. One by one we squinted through the new frames and gasped, "Hey, these make everything *double*." Mark's reaction was odder still. "With these, there's only *one* of everything. What's going on?" Gradually the truth dawned on us. When one looks through another's prism lenses the world is seen as if with their uncorrected vision. For thirteen years Mark had been seeing double . . . and none of us had had the faintest clue. Certainly not Mark.

As he put it, "I just figured that since we have two eyes, we ought to see two of everything. A long time ago I realized that the object on the left was the 'real' one, while the other was just its partner." What I wanted to blurt out at the moment was, "No wonder it was so hard for you to hit all those baseballs I pitched in the back yard!" In point of fact Mark had capably learned to read, to ride a bike, and to work out math problems in a duplex world. Most intriguing of all was his ultimate rejection of the glasses. "They make the world seem so empty — almost like a cartoon world." To this day he happily sees double.

From time to time God corrects my vision of the cosmos. At various moments, some dramatic and some subtle, God seems to announce, "This is what things really look like. This is reality because this is the way *I* see reality." My experience, however, is that I also do not easily wear new lenses. New vision plays havoc with my calendar. It necessitates reshuffling my values. It spoils my sermon plans. It keeps me up at night. I openly admit two things: There is nothing more exciting than a divinely provided glimpse of what actually *is*, and there is, simultaneously, nothing more ruinous to everything that brings me comfort.

My spiritual story and that of Zionsville Presbyterian Church are closely linked. I was the organizing pastor of this congregation on the suburban fringe of Indianapolis in 1983. I have experienced firsthand its faltering first steps, its seasons of growth and drought, and the

Spirit's persistent attempts to help us identify and embrace the vision of God's own choice.

Quite frankly we've resisted the vision. We've settled for many comfortable "second bests" until prodded, pushed, and forcibly compelled to have our spiritual eyesight checked. I believe that God has graciously cared for us and prepared us as each new part of the puzzle, each fresh wave of vision, has been presented for our response.

I am not a member of that small slice of the leadership pie that relishes radical change. Sit with me sometime at my favorite restaurant. Every time I go there I pick up the menu and read the descriptions of various entrees. Why do I do that? I've been to that restaurant at least seventy-five times, and I already know what I'm going to order. It's either going to be the Charleston salad or the chili. The server will come by the table and say, "We have a special today. It's Cajun fried orange roughy with sautéed vegetables." "Boy, that sounds great," I say. "I'll have the chili."

I've come to realize that most congregations prefer predictable entrees, no matter what God happens to be serving. The gravity of familiarity pulls us to the safety of tried-and-true patterns.

The development of our congregation reveals a similar tango of envisioning the future and reaching for the courage to embrace it. Our first fifteen years may be broken roughly into three five-year periods, in which our vision has been informed by decidedly different sources.

I wish I could help plant this church all over again . . . this time *on purpose*. Looking back, it's clear that our earliest vision was not so much purpose-centered as it was driven by the vagaries of demographics. Our church was established according to the Burger King model: that is, one look at the growing periphery of Indianapolis revealed that the northwest side needed a new outlet of our denominational franchise. If we built it they would come. And we all knew who "they" were — Presbyterians and other mainline churchgoers who' had moved into houses in the Zionsville area too far away to enjoy the long commute to their churches of origin.

Yes, our original mission statement appropriately hinted at the need to reach unchurched people. But none of us had any idea how to tackle such an ideal. We had never talked to unchurched people to learn what they were seeking. We eagerly and effectively organized a congregation that essentially amounted to a warm version of the church of our collective memory. We gave birth to a "family church" — a haven for convinced church attenders. Despite our functional ignorance of the Great Commission during those first five years, God graciously blessed us and Sunday attendance began to grow.

When we reached 250 worshipers each week I began to notice some changes. First of all, I was exhausted. Driven by the self-imposed expectation that every decision ought to cross my desk and every family room deserved my personal presence at least once a year, I began to despair that I would never escape the sensation of fatigue. Our growing congregation and growing guest list on Sunday mornings — combined with my growing family at home — began to overwhelm me. Increasingly I felt guilty every time I made a call or headed to the office. "I should be home right now," I reckoned. "What kind of husband and father am I?" Sitting at home I found myself thinking, "I should be out making calls tonight. What kind of pastor am I?" The frenzy of attempting to keep all the balls in the air at the same time and the accelerating anxiety of falling short both at home and at work began to crush me. I yearned for a different way to do church.

About the same time I began to notice that more than half of our attenders seemed to have ended up at the wrong franchise. They knew little or nothing of our denominational distinctiveness. Increasingly we attracted young families (born after World War II) who had no church pedigree whatsoever. Slowly we began to rethink our target audience. Instead of positioning our young congregation as a homing beacon for "our kind of people," we began to imagine what it would be like to make a dent in the 59 percent of Boone County residents who identified themselves as non-church attenders.

This realization hit home with special force one Sunday at the end of an Inquirers Class. In the presence of several dozen potential new members I fell on my pastoral sword, admitting shamefacedly that I hadn't yet made a home visit to a single one of them. I was shocked to see the palpable relief on their faces. "Oh, you don't need to do that," they assured me. "Why would you want to visit us, anyway?" They professed dread at the thought of having to clean up their family rooms to receive a guest. An unchurched inquirer stated meekly, "I have no idea what you'd expect me to say to you . . . or even to serve you as a snack!" A new world was dawning before my eyes, a world in which traditional pastoral expectations just might be set aside. These young new members weren't encumbered by the traditional notion that lay people were incapable of doing ministry. They expected to contribute. I began to ask myself, "How might we rethink our church so that everyone might make a difference?"

The result was a frenetically exciting second five years informed by a new vision — a vision of a permission-giving, decentralized ministry style, one that saw the termination of standing committees (which our members had generally experienced as fruitless and boring) and the arrival of dozens of small groups and ministries. Our emphasis shifted from the-pastor-does-it-all to a spotlight on the gifts and calling bestowed on every believer by the Holy Spirit. Scores of individuals moved from Sunday spectators to ministry players. Two of the outcomes of this new approach to ministry I had long assumed were mutually exclusive: multiplication of new members and less stress for the pastor. My work load actually lessened as the congregation tripled in size.

Indeed there were genuine reasons to celebrate. But with time, the poverty of our church's vision became gnawingly apparent. Yes, there were more people on site. They were certifiably more assimilated than ever. They were even being managed in a way that affirmed their gifts and calls. Christ, however, did not send his followers to manage, but to transform ordinary men and women into full-fledged disciples. I became haunted by our numbers, the very numbers that looked so good on the denominational spreadsheet. What had our growth accomplished? *We had multiplied the number of people who really had no clue how to obey Christ as Lord every hour of every day.*

Sequentially, our vision had been demographically driven and ministry-driven. How could it be driven by the Master's call to make disciples? On my watch a church had grown up in Zionsville, Indiana, filled with members who deeply admired Mother Teresa but had no idea how to *imitate* Mother Teresa. For that matter, my teaching and preaching had never seriously floated the notion that people

17

ought to be as devoted in body, mind, and spirit as that little Albanian nun. She was applauded by us all as a splendid aberration. During times of wrestling with God and in rereading the teachings of Jesus, I uncomfortably came to see that for ten years I had failed to challenge the American assumption that affluent Christians can enjoy the benefits of a life with God without seriously compromising their lifestyles.

Today our leadership team is working to demonstrate how all those called to our congregation might fulfill God's primary mandate: to become lifelong learners, or disciples, of Jesus Christ. We set before the congregation the ideal of *six marks of the disciple*. These include a heart for Christ alone, a mind transformed by the Word, arms of love, knees for prayer, a voice to speak the good news, and a spirit of sacrifice.

After years of upholding a model whereby a hundred believers send one of their number to "go be a missionary" on a foreign piece of geography, it's not easy to admit that we didn't quite get it right. What we meant to model was the sending of one of our number to be a *foreign* missionary — to learn a new language, to understand a local culture, to sacrifice the amenities of affluence, and to live knowing that he or she is always being watched by seekers — while the rest of us will stay here as lifetime *local* missionaries, learning to speak the language of the unchurched, understanding secular culture, sacrificing the amenities of affluence, and living as a "watched" person in a society that is skeptical of Christian spirituality until it sees the real thing on display.

QUESTIONS FOR REFLECTION AND DISCUSSION

1. To what extent do the characteristics of "old church" describe your congregation?
2. What is the vision that compels your church? How do you participate in this vision?
3. What does pastor McDonald's story say to you about your church?

4. How can individuals and officers in your congregation begin to imagine it as a Church in the Spirit? How can you help this process to occur?

CHAPTER TWO

The Community of Christ

NOTHING IS QUITE so amazing as the fact that we mortals should become the body of Christ, the "earthly form of his existence." The apostle Paul made the daring affirmation that "Now you are the body of Christ and everyone members of it" (1 Cor. 12:27). If we are truly his body, baptized persons have been infused with the presence of his Spirit. This Spirit, sacramentally imparted to us in baptism, affirmed in confirmation, and experienced in a variety of nurturing, life-giving ways, provides life to every congregation and empowers it for mission. For the church to be faithfully the church requires it to become aware of and responsive to the Spirit of Christ which is present in it.

A half-century ago Dietrich Bonhoeffer said, "The Church is Christ existing as community." What does this bold affirmation mean for a church seeking a vision of itself as the body of Christ? In a minimal sense it means the church embodies Christ. It suggests that he gives life and energy to the community. And, the communal "form of his existence" implies the church continues what Christ began. The community of Christ may be a very human gathering, but it is always more; it is a bearer of the holy.

To some extent this vision of a community inhabited by the Spirit of the risen Lord has been lost in the building of institutions. The dimension of the holy has too often been tamed and absorbed by the hu-

20

man, thereby inhibiting its spontaneous, unpredictable nature. As a consequence, the church as an organization has often become one more social institution alongside of others. Has this occurred in your congregation?

To personalize what this social institution feels like to an outsider, imagine the following letter being written after a desperate young man visited a cultural church.

Dear Mom,

I am writing to you about the experience I had in church this past Sunday. You always taught me that when I came to the end of my own strength, I should turn to God. Well, I came to the end of myself last week when Mary Louise asked me to move out of the house. We have been having pretty serious problems for the past year and it all came to a head when the company announced that I would again have to travel.

After sleeping in the guest room Saturday night, I awoke Sunday morning with the thought that I should go to church. I waited for Susan, who as you know is five years old, to wake up. I dressed her and we headed for the big church on the corner.

When we turned into the parking lot, I noted a lot of late model cars — Mercedes, Lexuses, BMWs. One of the professional greeters welcomed us, but before she had finished telling us how glad they were to have us, she turned and began speaking to an old-time member.

We seated ourselves and waited for the service to begin. Several families sitting around us seemed absorbed in conversation and one seemed prayerful. None of them spoke to us. The sermon was acceptable, I suppose, but most of it dealt with the capital campaign and how greatly the church needed funds. I waited, hoping there'd be something said about God or hope, but it never came.

After the sermon and before we were dismissed, the minister invited all who wished to join this church to come forward after the service. He emphasized how warm and friendly they were as a congregation and he reminded all the members to speak to those around them. Unfortunately, those around me must not have heard him.

On the way out of church I spoke to the minister and told him that I really would like to talk with him. He indicated that he would be away this week but I could call the week following. I got the impression that my problem was not too important to him.

As I walked toward the parking lot, I noticed a number of small clusters of folks talking with each other. They seemed to be quite happy to see each other but nobody reached out to us. Maybe I was just hurting too badly or maybe I'm too sensitive at this particular time. I had hoped to find help but didn't.

I hope you'll pray for us, Mom. I'd like to work it out with Mary Louise, but if I can't, I sure am going to need a community where I feel like I belong.

As always,
Sam

This imaginary experience captures the disappointment of many who have made their way into a church looking for help. Chances are pretty good that the people who ignored Sam are not selfish, uncaring persons. They are a group of nice people who are bound together with social glue, and they would be embarrassed to know that a person like Sam got ignored at a worship service. Even if they had spoken to him, they likely would not have been sensitive to the pain he felt, nor would they have known how to respond to it. In all likelihood they probably thought he was already a member, and questioned whether they should welcome him.

We have very good biblical reasons for thinking of the church as more than an institution, and something other than a gathering of nice people held together by cultural values. The scriptures of the New Testament provide ample grounding for our claim.

Seeing the Church as the Community of Christ

For the vision of the church as community we are indebted to a seriously conflicted first-century church. Isn't it strange how profound insights come from problematical situations? The church at Corinth caused Paul numerous, serious problems. To begin with, they chose sides against each other. One said "I belong to Paul," while another said "I am a disciple of Apollos."

This party spirit led to forbidden practices, law suits, and confusion about the nature of sacrifices offered to idols. Their striving, bickering, and dividing into power groups evoked from Paul the image of the church as the body of Christ.

As we explore the meaning of being "the body of Christ," it becomes obvious that "body" implies community. It is true that Christ dwells in each of us, but not all of Christ lives in any one of us. Because of this, the fullness of Christ can only be known in community. Paul's great metaphor of the "body" reminds us that no single one of us constitutes the body. Each is a member of the body but none is the whole body.

These are Paul's words:

> For just as the body is one and has many members, and all the members of the body, though many, are one body, so it is with Christ. For in the one Spirit we were all baptized into one body — Jews or Greeks, slaves or free — and we were all made to drink of one Spirit.
>
> Indeed, the body does not consist of one member but of many. If the foot would say, "Because I am not a hand, I do not belong to the body," that would not make it any less a part of the body. And if the ear would say, "Because I am not an eye, I do not belong to the body," that would not make it any less a part of the body.
>
> If the whole body were an eye, where would the hearing be? If the whole body were hearing, where would the sense of smell be? But as it is, God arranged the members in the body, each one of them, as he chose. If all were a single member, where would the body be?
>
> As it is, there are many members, yet one body. The eye cannot

say to the hand, "I have no need of you," nor again the head to the feet, "I have no need of you." On the contrary, the members of the body that seem to be weaker are indispensable, and those members of the body that we think less honorable we clothe with greater honor, and our less respectable members are treated with greater respect; whereas our more respectable members do not need this. But God has so arranged the body, giving the greater honor to the inferior member, that there may be no dissension within the body, but the members may have the same care for one another. If one member suffers, all suffer together with it; if one member is honored, all rejoice together with it.

Now you are the body of Christ and individually members of it. (1 Cor. 12:12-27)

Note the key phrase in this description, "the body is one and has many members." The contrast of the one with the many reveals both the unity and the diversity of the body of Christ, a united community with many different members. There is one body, the body of Christ, into which we are baptized. There is no Pauline body nor is there a body of Apollos.

The body metaphor provides Paul a way of dealing with the different power groups at Corinth. As the body has different parts and those parts do not have the same function, Christ has many members and they do not have the same function. But it is clear that all who belong to Christ participate in his body. No matter how great the differences, all are made one in Christ — Jews, Gentiles, slaves, free persons, male and female. The body of Christ rules out divisions on the basis of race, class, or gender. This insight holds great importance for a church that has formed itself along racial, economic, and social lines.

This one body, however, contains many different members who must resist forbidden practices. Members of the body cannot exclude themselves from the body; one member cannot be the whole body; members cannot function without a connection with the other members; and, members may not discount each other.

For example, a member of the body cannot exclude him or herself on the basis of function. The hand may say, "Because I am not the eye, I do not belong to the body," but this declaration does not remove the hand from the body. An eye cannot disconnect from the body because it is not a foot. God has placed each member in the body and has given each a particular function. For each member to discover his or her function in the body, and to accept that function, does indeed offer a practical basis for mutual love and acceptance. If every congregation could accept this principle, it would save itself from many divisive arguments.

Furthermore, Paul emphasizes that no one member can claim to be the whole body. "If the whole church were an eye, where would the hearing be?" If the church consisted of only one function, it would be void of the richness supplied by the variety of members. The question "What kind of church would Christ's church be, if every member of the church were just like me?" could truly be the occasion of a startling revelation.

In light of this intricately woven body, Paul concludes that it cannot function without the contribution of every member. In fact, he stresses the point that seemingly unnecessary members are just as important as those who appear to have greater importance. Every member has its place; every member has its function. No person in the church is worthless; each has his or her place to fill, role to play, gift to give. To a homogeneous congregation, this strongly suggests that members should pay attention to those who do not look like, think like, or smell like most of the present members. In a "look-alike church" it is not so much the outsiders who are the great losers but the insiders.

Finally, this metaphor of the body of Christ indicates that one member cannot discount another. Paul explicitly states, "Those members of the body that seem to be weaker are indispensable." Every member, even the weak and ugly ones, have an indispensable role to play.

Now, in this moment and in this place, we are the body of Christ. Those who believe in Christ, who have been baptized into him, who draw their life from him, who relate to all the others who are in him — we are the body of Christ. As his body we continue to do in our flesh what he began in his.

For the church to function effectively as the body of Christ, we have noted the urgency of a vision of the church as Christ's "earthly form of existence," but we equally require an understanding of community and how to evoke it in our congregations. The vision and its practical implementation point to complementary aspects of the body like inhaling and exhaling — inhaling a vision and exhaling new forms and practices. Without a vision the decisions and practices turn into utilitarian maneuvering, but without concrete practices the vision is empty idealism.

Two Aspects of Community

The creation and development of Christian community depend on two different structures, one formal and the other relational. These two aspects of community are clearly illustrated in the early formation of the church. On the day of Pentecost, Peter preached and three thousand persons believed his message and became the nucleus of the early church. Luke describes the event in these words:

> So those who welcomed his message were baptized, and that day about three thousand persons were added. They devoted themselves to *the apostles' teaching and fellowship, to the breaking of bread and the prayers.* Awe came upon everyone, because many wonders and signs were being done by the apostles. All who believed were together and had all things in common; they would sell their possessions and goods and distribute the proceeds to all, as any had need. Day by day, as they spent much time together in the temple, they broke bread at home and ate their food with glad and generous hearts, praising God and having the goodwill of all the people. And day by day the Lord added to their number those who were being saved. (Acts 2:41-47)

In the birth of the Acts church, the gospel was preached, the multitude heard, a large number responded, and the church was formed. Luke identifies four practices of this community: the apostles' teaching, fellowship, the breaking of bread, and the prayers. Two of these are formal aspects of community: the apostles' teaching and breaking bread. Two are relational: fellowship and the prayers. A vital community requires both the formal, which defines boundaries, worldview, and purposes; and the relational, which centers in fellowship and worship. A closer examination of the Acts community will make these two aspects clearer.

The formal aspects of the community in the early church sprang from the apostolic preaching and the sacraments of baptism and Eucharist. The preaching of the apostles centered in the coming of the kingdom in Jesus. Jesus is the Messiah who has been crucified, raised, and is coming again. He has set things right between God and humanity, and faith in him makes persons participants in this new program of God.

Preaching defined a new world for those who heard the message. Building on the Jewish vision of a Creator who called the world into being and created humans to participate in the divine purpose, the apostles proclaimed that the alienation between God and humans had been overcome in Jesus, that a new world order was being instituted, bridging the gap between Jews and Gentiles, slave and free, women and men. This proclamation defined a view of the world and provided the foundation of faith for this fledgling community. The Christian vision of reality defined the basis for their unity as a people.

The preaching of the apostles made the mission of this new community remarkably clear — to bear witness to the world of God's incursion into human history. On the eve of his departure Jesus had said to the apostles, "You will be my witnesses in Jerusalem, Judea, Samaria and to the ends of the earth" (Acts 1:8). In another setting he had commanded his followers "to make disciples of all nations, baptizing them in the name of the Father and of the Son and of the Holy Spirit" (Matt. 28:20). So, through the teaching of the apostles these early followers of the risen Christ soon realized their mission. Their purpose or goal or mission provided yet another formal aspect of their life in community.

In addition to the worldview and mission that stemmed from the apostles' preaching, the sacraments of baptism and Eucharist provided two formal practices germane to communal life. Baptism marked the entry into the community. It implied that persons had died, were buried with Christ, and in him were raised to new life. Baptism, to the early church, meant a new beginning, a new creation. From the standpoint of community, baptism marked those who belonged and those who did not.

Eucharist, the breaking of bread and the drinking of wine as the body and blood of Christ, provided a weekly rehearsal of his death and resurrection. But more than a remembrance, the ritual was indeed the continual reception of his life-giving presence into themselves. Through baptism they were joined to him in his death and resurrection; through Eucharist they were nurtured in their new life.

These formal aspects of community have a "thereness" about them. God, the Creator and Redeemer of the world, stands beyond the believer's grasp or control; God and the created world are a given. The mission of the church does not reside in the likes or dislikes of the community; it is given. The mission rests on the commission of Christ to "go into all the world." The effectiveness of baptism does not rest on the full understanding of the recipient either; it is efficacious in and of itself. The body and blood of Christ do not depend on the members of the community but on the power of God. So in formal, objective ways these structures and practices form the community of Christ.

Relational Aspects of Community

The text in Acts states, "They devoted themselves to the apostles' teaching and fellowship, to the breaking of bread and the prayers." The community requires formal aspects of its life that define, establish, and guide the followers of Christ; but it also needs internal practices that strengthen and nurture relationships. The relational aspects of community require fellowship and worship, and without this internal glue the congregation will eventually splinter with division, suffer loss of energy, and submerge individuality into the corporate membership. A dynamic community also depends upon the presence of Christ in ways that are personal and experiential.

While the church comes into being through the preaching of the

Word and celebrating the sacraments, the experience of relatedness occurs in the sharing of personal stories. As persons share their life stories, they listen for and hear elements of their own stories overlapping and blending with the stories of others. A feeling of relatedness to another's story creates a bond joining those who share the story. Through the sharing of life, both in stories and in suffering, the bonds of which St. Paul speaks become manifest in deep personal relationships.

Sharing narratives unites on several levels at once. On a cognitive level telling stories communicates a knowledge of each other. On an affective level storytelling evokes feelings of caring. On the communal level sharing stories creates an entity larger than those who hold the conversation; it creates community. And when members participate in mission together, shared stories are affirmed and deepened. In all these practical ways the community, which is the body of Christ, becomes concretized in particular congregations through storied relationships.

Sharing on all these levels provides affirmation, caring, and ministry, which cements together members of a congregation. Initial, formal connections may occur by joining a church, but they are deepened by telling life stories. These relations are immeasurably enriched by the love of others which flows through the sharing of life. A loving congregation freely offers affirmation and encouragement to strengthen the bonds of community, and until the members of the community experience this depth of caring, the unity of the body of Christ and the promised mutuality remain mere words.

In addition to sharing individual stories within the congregation, linking personal stories to the congregation's Master Story creates an even stronger bond between the members. Each congregation, like each member, has a story that it carries in its corporate memory. When an individual story gets connected with the congregation's Master Story, a deep sense of belonging occurs. On the other hand, a great deal of frustration and unhappiness occurs when personal narratives cannot be heard, affirmed, and incorporated into the congregation's ongoing story. This transcendent connection provides a reference for members and offers a greater and different kind of bonding from that achieved through the sharing of individual stories.

The Master Story is a powerful agent for unity and ministry, or it can become a deterrent to mission. A church's Master Story is a narrative composed by the community, based on their interpretation of the things that have happened to them. This Master Story resides in the collective memory of the church, and it controls, directs, distorts, or clarifies everything that happens in the corporate life of the particular congregation. These Master Stories are of different kinds and can both create and destroy, sap energy from or strengthen the community. Wise leadership always gets to know, appreciate, and affirm or challenge the Master Story.

The community finds an intimate bonding through the sharing of stories, but storied relations without the dimension of the Spirit create a merely human community. When, however, those who have shared stories gather to worship God, their fellowship is lifted to a transcendent level and their love and unity is sealed by the Spirit. These worshipful acts open the consciousness of the community to God, and an awareness of the divine presence joins them together in ways mere human sharing cannot.

Building Christian Community

In one sense we do not build Christian community, it is the gift of Christ. Community occurs when the baptized become aware of and responsive to their union with Christ. Baptism, as a sacrament, buries every member in the body of Christ and unites the baptized with every other baptized believer. But this sacramental action means very little in the formation of community until fellowship and worship actualize it.

In its most elementary form, community begins when one person listens to the story of another, when meeting occurs, when lives touch each other in openness. Community happens in meeting. The more significant the sharing, the deeper the experience of community. Christ is always present when stories are shared and the walls of separation are torn down, but his presence often goes unrecognized.

Community grows when two or three gather around Christ, reflecting on him and sharing their insights and longings. Reading the text of scripture together, exposing pain and sharing hope, exchanging insights and wisdom — all of this provides nurture for building a vital community.

Community solidifies through sharing tasks. When members of the community engage in ministry together, when they serve together or make pilgrimages together, community congeals. Not all persons have the gift of verbalizing their insights and feelings, even though they are deeply spiritual. These growing disciples of Christ often discover community by feeding the hungry or helping build a house for a homeless family. Healthy communities involve the whole person in knowing, sharing, and working together.

Community created in cell-like groups matures when it interfaces with other groups who have a different story and experience. These encounters include: reports of ministry, testimony to personal transformation, shared visions of the future and ways of mutual assistance.

Whether community occurs in one-to-one relationships, in small groups, in sharing tasks, or in interfacing with other groups, the vitality of these encounters comes from Christ. Encounters in multiple settings place us in a position to be open to him, to listen for him in the voice of another, and to share with him in the tasks he has for us to do in our time. In these numerous ways the church takes the form of his body on earth, and it continues his ministry in the world.

Transforming Power of Community

For mission to be effective, it must be grounded in a living community; otherwise it becomes good works without Christ, humanitarianism without spiritual grounding. But when the living presence of Christ takes shape in a particular community, it has an amazing power to transform the lives of those it touches and embraces. This expression of Christ in material form powerfully attracts persons to itself; it embraces diverse persons; it welcomes participation from outsiders and marginalized persons; and it transforms those it touches.

Community attracts attention without planning to. When a community alive to the Spirit of Christ gathers, amazing things happen: the deaf hear, the blind see, and the dead are raised up — transformations

31

that do not go unnoticed by the general populace. The community that worships in joy unites all who are alienated. When rich and poor, black and white, powerful and oppressed eat together, when the least have a place at the head table, when the community cares for its own and evokes the response of "See how they love one another" — when these things actually occur, the world takes notice. Values are reversed and worldviews are challenged.

The community of Christ embraces all kinds of persons and opens itself to change as they enter it. Human communities, homogeneous units, and socially selective groups cannot make these changes because their ground for unity resides in the values of the dominant culture, not in Jesus Christ. In exclusive gatherings, those who do not participate in the dominant culture feel unwelcome. But in the community of Christ, an inclusive fellowship, outsiders are welcomed — freed from oppression and transformed by being included.

In a vital community persons may inquire without being interrogated; from the outset, persons in their uniqueness are taken seriously. Easy, open-ended questions create safety and permit persons to share at their own level of comfort. Learning to ask enabling questions helps greatly in building a welcoming community.

Community transforms others because it invites participation in the corporate and individual activities it sponsors. Persons on the margin are changed by participating in celebration with persons at the center. This transforming power of a community has been described most clearly by the apostle Paul:

> If, therefore, the whole church comes together and all speak in tongues, and outsiders or unbelievers enter, will they not say that you are out of your mind? But if all prophesy, an unbeliever or outsider who enters is reproved by all and called to account by all. After the secrets of the unbeliever's heart are disclosed, that person will bow down before God and worship him, declaring, "God is really among you." What should be done then, my friends? When you come together, each one has a hymn, a lesson, a revelation, a tongue, or an interpretation. Let all things be done for building up. (1 Cor. 14:23-26)

Paul envisions a congregation in which all the members possess the Spirit, all share in the gifts of the Spirit, and the living Christ ministers through each of them. When persons encounter this vital worship, they meet Christ and they are convinced of his presence. In this manner the Christian community transforms those who come into it.

At all levels the congregation becomes a community of fellowship and discernment. The community of Christ has clear definition, boundaries that mark those who are inside and those outside. In this growing community, the way we experience Christ varies — knowledge of Christ, commitment to Christ, and being called and sent forth by Christ.

A Corroborating Witness

Advertising gurus are always in search of the million-dollar word: the single word on a package that will compel us to make a purchase, or to use more of a product than we intended. A few years ago a group of Madison Avenue observers ventured the opinion that the most successful million-dollar word ever devised appears on the back of shampoo bottles. At the end of those directions that tell us to wet our hair, work up a lather, and rinse away the bubbles, someone thought to add the word, "Repeat." An awful lot of shampoo has emerged from millions of bottles as a result.

Is there a million-dollar word in the New Testament's account of the early church? I believe the best candidate is "together." Acts 2:44 says, *"All the believers were together and had everything in common."* Two sentences later we read, *"Every day they continued to meet together in the temple courts. They broke bread in their homes and ate together with glad and sincere hearts."* Together, Jesus' friends survived their ups and downs. Together they discovered God's resources to change the world. Together they approached their heartbreaks, their jobs, their marriages, their fears, and their problems. If the example of the early church is at all normative, God's people are called to do things together that we could never do by ourselves.

Entering a shared life challenges us to live and move and have our being in a culture that screams for the absolute priority of radical individualism. Today the availability of personal choices for one's vocation, spirituality, sexual partners, and soft drink brands isn't heralded as mere possibility, but as an inalienable right.

People who live along the suburban fringe of Indianapolis desperately want to be in relationships that matter, but intuitively believe that making commitments to others may threaten their personal freedom. Besides, will other people even be there tomorrow? Twenty percent of Americans relocate every year. We do not know our neighbors. I may know more about Jay Leno's likes, dislikes, and hobbies than I know about the man who lives three doors from me.

It's ironic that at the end of the twentieth century the institution that has been philosophically discarded by so many — the church — embodies the brightest hope for satisfying our culture's gnawing hunger for community. In churches people can come *together,* in real time and real space, to touch and be touched, to forgive and to seek healing, and to become part of a unique, progressively unfolding story that is being authored by the Spirit of God. In churches everywhere the Spirit's strategy for generating this experience of community seems increasingly related to small groups.

I'm convinced that the viable and life-transforming congregation of the future will be a church *of* small groups, not merely a church *with* small groups. In other words, covenant partnerships with a few other people won't be presented as a side dish on the church's menu; they will be identified as the essential strategy for fulfilling congregational mission.

What are small groups? They are intentional face-to-face gatherings of three to fourteen people, meeting at least once each month (preferably two, three, or four times) for the primary purpose of discovering and growing together in the abundant life of Jesus Christ.

The rationale for these mini-communities has always been part of the Christian story. Jesus taught the crowds, partnered in ministry with the Seventy, but discipled and shared life with the Twelve. Healthy small groups are clearly the best way for contemporary Christians to express and experience the fifty-eight "one another" references in the

New Testament. (Would it really be wise to aggressively pursue "Admonish one another" and "Confess your sins to each other" in the setting of one hundred and fifty people at Sunday worship?)

Small groups are a preferred way of helping prevent a church from growing colder as it grows larger. By valuing relationships, these groups reflect a greater commitment to people than to tasks. The old paradigm for church life can be summarized, "We get together to get things done, and use people to make it happen." The Church in the Spirit must affirm, "We get together to build each other up, and the kingdom comes about as a consequence."

Today nearly half of those involved in Zionsville Presbyterian Church are folded into one or more of 120 small groups. They can be roughly classified into three species: *round* groups that focus on study, shared spiritual life, and accountability; *square* groups that center on tasks, mission endeavors, and/or governance; and *triangular* groups that prioritize an experience of shared prayer and support.

For several years we actively pursued a standardization of group life at our church — trying to make leaders and participants jump through the same behavioral hoops. Today we better understand the complexity of our church's social culture. The Spirit has woven together a variety of people with differing social, emotional, and spiritual needs. Some individuals drawn to groups appreciate structure; others crave spontaneity. Some participants are in need of learning the ABC's of Christian faith; others are ready to wade through deeper waters. Some group members are eager to serve; others are looking to give or to receive intensive care. Abandoning our myopic fixation on one kind of group has allowed us to enjoy the diversity of these small gatherings that have been so richly used by God.

Group life was not a key component of our church's original vision. Its value and its urgency only gradually dawned on us. Our initial efforts to form groups and invite participation were clumsy at best. With considerable passion I issued a "Cattle Call" to the congregation: "If you truly want the best that God has in store for your life, put your name on the small group sign-up sheet *today*." The results were immediate — more than fifty curious souls obliged — but the effort was ultimately disastrous. I didn't realize that availability to meet on Saturdays at 10:00 A.M. was far too weak a bond to keep ten people together for more than a few months. Three of the first five groups we organized soon disintegrated, and the other two eventually merged.

With time it became clear that the key currency in a small group-oriented church is lay leadership. The presence of a called, trained, and encouraged leader makes more difference to the viability and health of a group than any other factor. Over the years the one method of group creation that has worked better for us than any other has been the identification of a leader or lead couple, who invite others into a shared experience. New members end up sampling and staying in particular small groups for the same reason people are drawn to particular churches: they are invited by people they already know and trust.

There has never been a single day, however, in which we have enjoyed a surplus of leaders. Our leader motor always seems to be about two quarts low. Rather than assembling some of the dozens of adults on our small group waiting list into ill-conceived and poorly led huddles, we've prayed for the patience and the skills to call "rising leaders" into the adventure of assuming the shepherd's role for ten other people. This has never been an easy task. At times the Spirit draws out three or four individuals who are obviously divinely energized and available to lead. At other times the leadership nursery has a population of zero. We keep plodding ahead, however, in the dual confidence that (1) the task of developing new leaders *cannot* be set aside, except at our peril, and (2) God is ultimately responsible for calling members of the body into ministry . . . and God will do so.

What comprises sufficient instruction for group leadership? Over the years we have offered several versions of "turbo training," which amounts to a crash course in basic skills. This provides for rapid dissemination of information and rapid deployment of new leaders, but unfortunately compels the trainees to take a mighty leap from the classroom to a real live group. Sometimes we've looked back and realized we provided a "crash" course indeed. Far better is the strategy of placing the rising leader or leader couple in the presence of an experienced mentor, so for up to a year they can watch and learn "on the job" in the context of a functioning group.

There is a particularly exciting role available for the pastor or skilled lay person: becoming a Johnny Appleseed, a mentor-leader who forms a short-term relationship with a group of prospective leaders. For a period of six to twelve months these couples and/or individuals (all personally recruited by a mentor, who promises to pour into them his/her wealth of experience in exchange for their prayerful consideration of becoming leaders) meet together as a small group. Everyone takes a turn at leadership under the watchful eye of the mentor. At the designated time for closure, the uniquely qualified mentor provides guidance and discernment from the Spirit in releasing these potential servants, or recommends further training or a different ministry altogether. Like Johnny Appleseed moving on to sow yet another orchard, the mentor is then free to recommence the process with another group.

A network of healthy small groups cannot be whipped up from a ministry cookbook. The specific leaders who are called forth and the varying speeds of transitioning an older or younger congregation to this kind of community experience must be taken into account, and there must be a profound dependence on the Spirit's work in a local context. But the costs along the way are vastly outweighed by the gains. As Paul writes to the Corinthians, "Don't you (plural in Greek) know that you yourselves are God's temple?" The Acts and the epistles never contemplate the existence of a solitary believer. It is *together*, not individually, that we will comprise the sanctuary in which a holy God will be pleased to dwell.

QUESTIONS FOR REFLECTION AND DISCUSSION

1. When visitors come to your church, do they experience it as "Christ existing as community" or like the young man who felt alienated and unnoticed?
2. Name the different groups in your church. How are these diverse groups held together when differences arise?
3. What are the formal and relational aspects of your church? How do they serve to nurture and unify persons? With which are you more comfortable?

4. Recall persons you have seen changed through the power of your Christian fellowship. How do you explain this phenomenon? Would small groups help you with this piece of the church's mission? How could your church initiate the process of small group formation?

CHAPTER THREE

Initiation in a Church
in the Spirit

H OW NEW PERSONS are received into the church signals to them
the church's faith, mission, and sense of purpose. Those initiated
into the body of Christ with an understanding of the faith and a clear
sense of the church's expectations will more likely become zealous,
committed members. On the other hand, if a church lacks clarity
about its mission, seeks members to prop up a sagging budget, and
does not communicate a challenging vision, it will reproduce more of
the same kind of members it already has. For too long, mainline
churches have multiplied social members without seeking their spiritual transformation.

A Church in the Spirit can ill afford a casual or haphazard initiation of members. If we continue to bring into the church persons who
do not know Christ and have no instruction in the life of the Spirit, we
dilute the membership and make the task of transformation almost impossible. Besides, the best and easiest place to begin creative change is
with those who are entering the church for the first time.

Initiation in the Cultural Church

A single description of a typical initiation into a mainline congregation will have numerous exceptions. Our aim is to depict several of those "less than adequate" practices of initiating new members so characteristic of many congregations. How do they receive new persons into the church?

One of the worst examples I know of involved an adolescent boy. "I went to church with my friend," he said. "We were sitting in the front row, and the minister signaled us to come to the front where he was standing. I thought he was asking us to receive the offering. When my friend and I sat down we'd been received into the membership of the church."

Slightly more acceptable than this surprise tactic is the sort of case in which a person needs only ask the minister for a membership transfer. The next day the minister mails a request for membership to the designated church, and the new person is counted a member.

In another situation, a person joining a particular church may be requested to meet with the governing body. The interview tends to be social rather than theological, and conversation about personal faith, the centrality of Christ, or the mission of the church seems never to be included. Joining the church becomes an act of social acceptance. In churches that receive members in this casual way, the persons being received are seldom asked about the meaning of being a Christian or about participating in the church's mission.

Other congregations conduct "new member orientations" for those joining the church. Generally, this orientation includes information about the particular denomination and its special emphases, an orientation to the particular congregation, an introduction to the pastor, and an opportunity to make a financial pledge. Again, there is no challenge to personal discipleship, nor any hint that the church has high expectations of persons entering its membership.

More intentional congregations conduct new member training that includes the basics of the faith, the mission of the church in the world, the church's expectations of new members, and a challenge to faithful discipleship. I believe this form of initiation into the church holds greater promise, but often the congregation into which the persons are being received remains in bondage to the values of the culture. This highly intentional form of initiation needs to go a step further and challenge the status quo with the radical demands of the gospel.

New members should be made aware that the present-day church will continue to undergo serious changes as the twenty-first century begins. The orientation and initiation into the church should include the meaning of discipleship and perhaps a challenge to participate in the movement of God into the new era when changes in worship, ministry, and lay involvement are likely to occur. The style of Jesus and the practices of the early church provide good material to nurture the creative imagination.

Jesus and His Disciples

In our search for help in preparing persons for membership, perhaps it would be instructive to examine the way that Jesus initiated his followers. Though we may not imitate his exact style, it will provide us basic, tested principles of initiation. A review of Jesus' early ministry is highly suggestive. In creating the original community, Jesus depended on the witness of John the Baptist to awaken interest in the kingdom movement he was proclaiming.

> The next day he saw Jesus coming toward him and declared, "Here is the Lamb of God who takes away the sin of the world! This is he of whom I said, 'After me comes a man who ranks ahead of me because he was before me.' I myself did not know him; but I came baptizing with water for this reason, that he might be revealed to Israel." (John 1:29-31)

John's witness awakened interest in several of his own disciples, and two of them followed Jesus to inquire about his identity. For the better part of an afternoon, they talked with Jesus and asked him about himself. Doubtless, Jesus answered all their questions in a satisfactory manner because they soon began following him.

41

When Jesus turned and saw them following, he said to them, "What are you looking for?" They said to him, "Rabbi" (which translated means Teacher), "where are you staying?" He said to them, "Come and see." They came and saw where he was staying, and they remained with him that day. It was about four o'clock in the afternoon. One of the two who heard John speak and followed him was Andrew, Simon Peter's brother. He first found his brother Simon and said to him, "We have found the Messiah" (which is translated Anointed). (John 1:38-41)

After this introduction to Jesus and his message of the kingdom, Jesus was walking by the sea of Galilee and called Peter and Andrew, James and John to become his followers and participate in his mission. They left everything to follow him.

Now after John was arrested, Jesus came to Galilee, proclaiming the good news of God, and saying, "The time is fulfilled, and the kingdom of God has come near; repent, and believe in the good news." As Jesus passed along the Sea of Galilee, he saw Simon and his brother Andrew casting a net into the sea — for they were fishermen. And Jesus said to them, "Follow me and I will make you fish for people." And immediately they left their nets and followed him. As he went a little farther, he saw James the son of Zebedee and his brother John, who were in their boat mending the nets. Immediately he called them; and they left their father Zebedee in the boat with the hired men, and followed him. (Mark 1:14-20)

After he called these followers, he demonstrated to them the power of the kingdom message when he cast the evil spirit out of the man in the synagogue. A pattern is developing in his manner of initiation: witness, information, call to leave all, and the demonstration of power.

They were astounded at his teaching, for he taught them as one having authority, and not as the scribes. Just then there was in their synagogue a man with an unclean spirit, and he cried out, "What have you to do with us, Jesus of Nazareth? Have you come to destroy us? I know who you are, the Holy One of God." But Jesus rebuked him, saying, "Be silent, and come out of him!" And the unclean spirit, convulsing him and crying with a loud voice, came out of him. They were all amazed, and they kept on asking one another, "What is this? A new teaching — with authority! He commands even the unclean spirits, and they obey him." (Mark 1:22-27)

Next, Jesus taught his disciples the meaning of his words. He taught the multitudes in parables but when they were alone he explained his teaching to his disciples. Speaking his message and having people understand his purpose were intrinsic to Jesus' way of initiating disciples into the community of faith. Here is one example:

"Listen! A sower went out to sow. And as he sowed, some seed fell on the path, and the birds came and ate it up. Other seed fell on rocky ground, where it did not have much soil, and it sprang up quickly, since it had no depth of soil. And when the sun rose, it was scorched; and since it had no root, it withered away. Other seed fell among thorns, and the thorns grew up and choked it, and it yielded no grain. Other seed fell into good soil and brought forth grain, growing up and increasing and yielding thirty and sixty and a hundredfold." And he said, "Let anyone with ears to hear listen!"

When he was alone, those who were around him along with the twelve asked him about the parables. And he said to them, "To you has been given the secret of the kingdom of God, but for those outside, everything comes in parables." (Mark 4:3-11)

After Jesus had demonstrated the message and taught his disciples, he then sent them out to participate in the ministry.

He called the twelve and began to send them out two by two, and gave them authority over the unclean spirits. He ordered them to take nothing for their journey except a staff; no bread, no bag, no money in their belts; but to wear sandals and not to put on two tunics. He said to them, "Wherever you enter a house, stay there until

you leave the place. If any place will not welcome you and they re-
fuse to hear you, as you leave, shake off the dust that is on your feet
as a testimony against them." So they went out and proclaimed that
all should repent. They cast out many demons, and anointed with
oil many who were sick and cured them. (Mark 6:7-13)

Jesus' manner of making disciples and uniting them in a community can be summed up in a few cardinal principles. You may wish to
create your own list, but consider this one:

- Personal witness awakens interest in Jesus. In this instance John
  the Baptist's witness provoked interest in his disciples. How
  might personal testimony be employed to awaken a person's interest in Christ and membership in his body?
- Questions about Jesus are dealt with face to face. Jesus invited
  John's awakened disciples to the place where he happened to be
  dwelling. In an intimate setting (a cave? a house? under a tree?)
  he answered their questions and spoke of his vision. What does
  this suggest to us about ways of providing information about the
  faith?
- Challenge disciples (learners) to follow Jesus. After spending
  time with John's disciples, Jesus issued a specific challenge to
  them to leave everything behind and follow him. How might we
  issue specific challenges to follow Jesus?
- Model effective ministry. Soon after Jesus called disciples to follow him, he entered a synagogue and cast an evil spirit out of a
  man. He demonstrated to his followers how to do ministry. How
  might we teach persons how to minister through hands-on experience?
- Teach new disciples the faith. As the disciples traveled with Jesus,
  he taught them kingdom principles. Perhaps his demonstrations
  of the kingdom evoked their questions and provided the opportunity for instruction. Does this action/reflection model of training suggest new ways of preparing persons to participate in the
  body of Christ?
- Send disciples into the kingdom mission. Those who began fol-

lowing Jesus were sent into the world to proclaim the kingdom in word and deed. The task of initiation is never finished until disciples are also missionaries. How do we help persons identify their gifts and discern their call?

The invitation of Jesus that transformed fishermen and tax-collectors into kingdom witnesses and leaders provides the contemporary congregation with powerful symbols to reimagine its mode of initiation. Each of these principles in the ministry of Jesus provides metaphor-like material to stimulate our intuition and inspire our imagination. Through the creative energy of the Holy Spirit, our congregations can reimagine for our time powerful initiation rites such as Jesus used long ago.

If we are to imagine initiation of new persons into the fellowship of the church in new and fresh ways, a number of issues must receive attention: the settings from which persons come to the church, the best methods, and the discernment of gifts.

Today's Visitors to the Church

Today missiologists look upon the United States as a mission field, a culture no longer permeated with the language and values of the church. The culture from which new persons come into the church provides little or no preparation for membership. In the next few decades, the North American culture will likely become more and more estranged from its Christian roots, and possibly even hostile to the faith. A society that once proclaimed the authority of God will likely repress Christian affirmations in public life, silence Christian witness in the halls of justice, demand taxes from churches, and repeal deductions of financial contributions. Hopefully, these antagonisms will not develop, but even if the culture remains neutral, the church should not expect help in forming persons spiritually from the outside.

In this new mission field, persons lack even a rudimentary knowledge of the gospel. Many will even need a definition of the word *Bible,* and especially the message it contains. But even worse, many

45

secular seekers will have corrupted ideas of God, the church, and the meaning of spiritual life. To assume they can enter the life of the church and be responsible members without instruction and training will be a gross mistake and perhaps the height of self-delusion.

To equip these persons to recognize signs of the kingdom and to participate in the larger ministry of the church, it is critical that we imagine more effective ways of bringing them into the fellowship of Christ's people. New members need a knowledge of the basics of the faith; they require experiences of community; they should be challenged with high expectations. They deserve, moreover, a significant role in the kingdom work. Persons will increasingly attend the church and participate before they become members. In order to become a member of the church they must demonstrate a seriousness of intention to follow Christ.

Vital Aspects of Initiation

Initiation into the church requires first and foremost a living community of faith to which an outsider can be joined. If there is no life in the mother, how can there be life in the child? Our discussion of the body of Christ as community clearly illustrates this point.

Before being received into the membership of the church, prospective members should show signs of a spiritual awakening or spiritual life. This suggestion does not mean the church should become legalistic in defining experiences that qualify persons for membership, nor should the church become a detective searching for evidence against faith. Rather, we are affirming that the church can define criteria for membership that include a desire to belong to the community of Christ; it can observe whether these desires translate into behaviors that give validity to the confession of those seeking membership. We must rid ourselves of the search for members for the sake of numbers only, and we must aim to help those received into membership find a vital, transformative faith.

The church will encounter multiple signs of awakening. These will include an interest in Christ and his mission, a searching spirit, a testimony to a spiritual encounter, and a concern about the meaning of life. Some may be drawn to God through the state of the world or by Christian acts of compassion or an association with church members or Christian groups. Still others may be awakened by a personal crisis that creates a hunger for a greater reality than they have known. A thousand other experiences may cause a person to awaken from slumber and begin to search for the spiritual dimensions of life.

A person who manifests one or more of these traits would likely be a good person to begin the process of initiation. Without these characteristics the intention to join the church often springs from social aspirations, with little evidence that the individual has been touched by the Spirit of God. The church's setting for mission in a pagan culture and the present state of the church clearly point to the necessity for a new type of member who has received careful training for membership.

The culture of the church forms the vision, values, and lifestyle of new members. By culture we mean the atmosphere, the climate, the accepted ways of being in a particular church, and the way that a congregation does ministry. For example, Baptist congregations function with a congregational form of government; each member feels both the privilege and responsibility of participating in the governance of the community. Since most Baptist congregations consider themselves evangelical, winning persons to Christ ranks high on the list of priorities. Thus, the educational program and the worship services emphasize the importance of witnessing to friends and neighbors. This emphasis leads to a way of life for the membership. All these values and the consequent lifestyle constitute the culture of a Baptist congregation.

A Presbyterian church in contrast may also recognize the significance of Christian witness, but it also feels compelled to work for the transformation of the culture and the elimination of injustices. These values will permeate the culture of a Presbyterian church like the evangelical passion pervades the Baptist congregation. A congregation may be a Church in the Spirit with either of these visions of mission, so long as it is grounded in the presence of the living Christ. Congregations rooted in Christ can have different gifts and different callings and thus different identities. Faithfulness, however, demands that they be guided by Christ and not by the values and norms of the culture.

A similar analysis can be made of other denominations, and of the congregations within each denomination. These different cultures exert enormous, often unconscious, influence on those who participate in them. With respect to initiation into membership, the culture of a particular congregation will have either a powerfully formative effect or a paralyzing, stultifying effect. Because of this communal power, it is critical for the congregation to stay clearly focused on Jesus Christ as the center and source of its life so that its culture manifests his kingdom rather than the values of a secular world. Furthermore, the culture of a congregation must support the initiation given new members, lest it become a deterrent to their transformation in Christ.

Since the church is Christ's body on earth, the various forms of initiation aim to help members be related to Christ and to discover their place in the community. Consider these questions about initiation. Do you not think that a personal relationship with Christ and the birth of awareness of his living presence would be an important emphasis in initiation? If the church is his body and every member is baptized into him, entrance into the community should be marked by claiming this relationship. Without question a relationship with Christ is important when anyone enters the church, but as we have indicated, this value should also be supported by the congregation's culture. If the initiation emphasizes a relationship with Christ, but members of the congregation feel embarrassed to speak of Christ or to support the new member in a lifestyle of faithfulness, spiritual schizophrenia quickly develops.

Those entering the congregation should have knowledge of the person of Christ. Since they are becoming part of his body on earth, they need a rich supply of images of who he was, what he did, and what he taught. These images of the Christian life can be derived from the Gospels. Perhaps initiation should provide help in understanding the Bible and its message for today.

Initiation will also include teaching about spiritual gifts. Discerning one's gifts may take time, but persons entering the church should know they possess gifts, and that these gifts are for ministry to others. The picture is both beautiful and appealing. When Christ through the gift of the Holy Spirit created his body at Pentecost, each member received a gift, a capacity to do what Christ had done. No one member had all the gifts but each had at least one, and when this one gift was joined with the other gifts in the body, Christ was made present to the world. Amazingly, Christ is still alive in the world today and continues his ministry through his body.

A deliberate aspect of initiation also focuses on finding a connection with other members of the body of Christ. At the entry point, members of Christ's body need to realize that the Christian life is not a solo sung in one's own key, but an anthem that blends their voice with others. The sense of community is most often experienced by making connections with other baptized persons. In this fellowship of faith each derives strength and encouragement from the other, and in these relations a person discovers the meaning of "being members one of another."

Initiation must include knowledge of a particular church's story — how it came to be, its life to this point, the particularity of the denominational relationship. Each congregation lives out a story constructed by its interpretation of the things that have happened in its life. These interpretations of events, like the call of the first minister, the building of the sanctuary, a fire, or the death of an influential member — all these become significant aspects of the church's story and its identity. If new members do not know the story, they will feel excluded from the life and decision making of the congregation.

This discussion of initiation has aimed to make clear the overlap between receiving new members and the creation of community. Obviously, individuals are joined to a community, and the uniting cannot occur unless there is a community to join. Furthermore, if this is a vital community, initiation should be of a nature that enhances the community.

Methods of Initiation

With the assumptions that we are making about the nature of the culture, the image of the initiate, and the role of the church, an important choice will be the methods of initiation. Those coming into the church lack the rudiments of Christian faith and ethics, and those who help them find a place in the fellowship cannot ignore this need. Since the manner in which persons enter the church defines their expectations, their loyalty, and the seriousness of their growth, our methods should be developed with care. For new members to achieve these positive benefits in their lives, they require not only instruction in the basics of the faith, but also interpersonal experiences of the faith.

Perhaps we could learn from the early church ways of initiating persons into the faith. In the first two centuries, membership in the church was not easy, nor was it automatic. Sometimes it took as long as a year or two years for admission into full membership. When a person indicated a desire to be baptized into this new faith, the church assigned a mentor to instruct the candidate in the faith. Seekers were allowed to attend worship until the mystery of the Eucharist was celebrated, at which time they had to leave. Persons in training for membership regularly met with their mentor to learn the Christian lifestyle. The emphasis fell much harder on lifestyle than on doctrine, and when the mentor judged that the candidate knew sufficiently how to live as a Christian, he recommended him or her for baptism.

Baptisms occurred at Easter. The candidate fasted for three days before Easter. The night before Easter Sunday was spent in prayer. At sunrise all those who had been prepared for baptism met in the church, stripped off their old garments, waded into the pool and were baptized by the bishop. When they came out of the pool, they were clothed in a white robe, symbolic of their new life. Those assisting with the sacrament gave the new Christians honey, salt, and milk symbolic of the fruit of the promised land, the seasoning of the earth, and the nurture of the Word of God. When the ritual was completed, the newly baptized could join the congregation in saying, "Our Father . . . ," a practice heretofore denied them. All the members of the congregation embraced and welcomed them into the fellowship.

Merely repeating this ancient ritual would not achieve the desired results for us today, but we can begin to imagine new ways of preparation and more effective ways of initiating persons into the fellowship through inspiration derived from the early church. A person entering the church should be interviewed in a manner that explores the candidate's life, background, and religious history. The interview might begin with simple, non-threatening questions like "How long have you lived in this area? What other places have you lived before moving here (if he or she is not a native of the area)? What kind of work do you do? Will you tell me about your family? What are some of the things you remember from your early years?" After exploring these data, you might ask questions about the person's religious background. "What has been your experience in or with the church? Have there been times in your life when God seemed very near to you? What are some of the things that you hope for in becoming a member of this congregation?"

Questions like these should be asked in an interesting, non-threatening manner to enable persons to speak naturally about their lives. Because listening has become a lost art in the "hurry up" society, most persons eagerly talk when given an opportunity. Spiritually sensitive persons can make the conversation a vital growth experience for the person telling her story.

Early in the initiation, introduce new persons to the Christian life as a journey. Helping them identify marker events of their lives will assist them in seeing the providence of God. Asking candidates for membership to identify the turning points in their lives often proves helpful. A turning point occurs when life has flowed in one direction until a particular thing happens. Because of this event, life takes a sudden turn in a new direction. For example, I was reared in a rural area until I was nine years old and then moved to town. Life seemed very much of a piece until that move — visits with relatives, going to school, waiting for my father to come home. After the move to town I had to make new friends, visit with another set of relatives, and attend a different school. This marker event closed one era of my life but it opened another.

Marker events provide the substructure of our life story and the implicit narrative contains our interpretation of the things that have happened to us throughout our life. With a bit of reflection, persons seeking membership can often identify God's presence in their unfolding story. When this occurs, it suddenly dawns upon them that their natural story is the carrier of their spiritual story.

When initiates into the community of faith begin to see their lives as a journey contained in a story, their wondering about the action of God in their lives enables them to name times when God was near. Seeing one's life as the "play ground of God" sensitizes persons and deepens their awareness of the spiritual aspects of their life stories. Wonder often evokes an awareness of the Spirit of God in the natural events of their lives. So invite persons to wonder about the persons who have influenced them, the persons who have strangely entered into their lives, or the persons they have admired. They may also wonder about why they decided to come to church or take an interest in the church or what caused them to consider the new member training. Wonder has a marvelous power to activate the imagination and open the door between the natural events of life and their spiritual depths.

Initiation will also include sharing stories of one's life. When persons have identified the marker events of their lives and have wondered about the things that have become part of their story, they can more easily talk about their lives. Training for membership will provide a setting in which to tell life stories. Sharing the story clarifies it for the storyteller and the story also provides material for bonding. This sharing creates community.

These questions may be helpful in calling forth this kind of sharing:

- What aspects of the Christian life have you seen demonstrated in two or three other persons? How have these persons modeled a Christian life for you?
- What has impressed you about Jesus Christ? When has he seemed the most real to you?
- How have you dealt with painful experiences? Whom have you had to forgive? Whom have you not forgiven?
- What is the question with which you are living today?

New members of the church will benefit from spending time with church leaders so they may share their faith with them. Likewise the new persons need to hear the faith of the leaders and their vision for the church.

The awakening and growth from the new member preparation will be strengthened through an ongoing small group. Make it clear that these groups will help each new member continue to grow in faith. When persons come into the church they are most open to change and growth.

A church with a number of mature Christians may wish to develop mentors and spiritual guides to companion new persons. The Christian faith is better caught than taught; get those who are mature in the faith in contact with those who wish to grow in the faith.

The Discernment of Gifts

Discerning gifts is far more than checking a list of time and talents. Discernment of gifts has a clear focus on the God who created these particular persons and gave them gifts. Also, discernment is about the Holy Spirit who gives special capabilities to the people of God. Discernment seldom comes instantaneously, but requires life to be lived in a community over a period of time.

We are clear that the task of the church is to proclaim, embody, and call forth the kingdom of God. Members of the church have the gifts to carry this ministry forward. But who does this work? Those who have received the gifts for ministry.

Certainly, an initial discernment can begin during the weeks of initiation. Explore with the members the things they like to do. The things they do best. The things that other persons tell them they do well. All these responses from self and others hint at the gifts that persons have. We most often perform well when we have gifts that match the task. When we enjoy what we do well, our gifts begin to be exposed. The contrary is also true. Persons dread doing what they do not have gifts to do.

Because of both these performance and emotional factors, invite persons into a ministry that utilizes their gifts. When we do not properly discern a person's gifts, we engage him or her in tasks that become sheer drudgery. This mismatch leads to discontent, burnout, and reluctance to respond to another call.

Small groups provide an excellent environment for the discernment of gifts. The groups formed during the weeks of initiation can be invited to reflect on questions like these:

1. What are the things that you have done well, things that you enjoy and feel natural to you? The use of your gifts makes tasks easy and brings delight.
2. What do other persons commend you for? What do they see in you and think that you do well? They may see gifts of which you are not aware.
3. What are the dreams that drive your life? If you had no restraints or limitations, what would you like most to do with your life? Your dreams point to your unrealized but real possibility, and likely the direction of your calling.

This exploration of initiation challenges the bland, cultural manner in which we have recruited new members. Examining the model Jesus used helps us imagine creative and effective ways of initiation today. Drawing on these resources and suggestions will provide a way to begin developing new models of welcoming persons into Christ's body and his ministry.

A Corroborative Witness

"Membership has its privileges," according to the marketing slogan of a popular credit card. What are the privileges of formal affiliation with a local church? Or as one inquirer asked me, "What do I get if I join?"

The first time I replied to that question I surprised myself with the sheer dullness of my answer. Presbyterian church members are empowered to vote at called meetings of the congregation and are eligible for election and ordination as deacons and elders. Aside from a few esoteric privileges of jurisprudence, that's about it. The pastoral secret of course is that the traditional "gains" of membership chiefly belong to the church. *Now we get to count you in our annual report, your name has been added to our stewardship campaign files, we have a license to canvass you to teach Sunday school, and from now on you can't slip away from church involvement without serious pangs of guilt.*

While the consumer-driven focus on privileges is disheartening, the "soft sell" heard by countless thousands exploring church membership is truly tragic. What are the *responsibilities* of membership? Years ago as I spoke farewells to those who had attended the last session of a particular Inquirers Class — the very meeting in which I sought to "close the deal" of bringing new members on board — I noticed that two young couples stayed behind, talking intently with each other. Neither of these couples had ever belonged to a congregation. They looked worried.

"Can I answer any questions for you?" I asked. "Well," they stammered, "we're not quite sure we're ready to make such a huge commitment."

"What's troubling you exactly?" I replied.

"There's attendance, for one thing," said one of the husbands. "I'm not sure we can be here every Sunday of the year."

"Oh, don't worry about that!" I assured them. I watched the tension flee from their faces as I described what amounted to the *least common denominator* of church involvement — the kind of behavior in God's people to which I had accommodated myself years earlier.

They smiled. They joined the church. They participated irregularly.

I wish I could have a second shot at that conversation. I wish I had been wise enough to honor the genuine tension in their faces and their sincere contemplation of perfect attendance for the Lord. It occurred to me about that time that the Zionsville Rotary Club was asking me to make a greater commitment of involvement — and promising swift retribution if I fell short — than I had ever dreamed of demanding of church members. *And I was the leader of the community pledged to transform human history.*

The more our congregation intentionally focused on discipleship, the more it was necessary to rethink, at a fundamental level, the meaning of membership. For several years I found myself torn between two parables. On the one hand Jesus declares that his followers are to be a city set on a hill. Shadowy, half-hearted disciples need not apply. This is the parable of exclusiveness. Jesus also describes the kingdom as a dragnet that ensnares everything within reach. The angels will separate the trout from the carp at the end of the age. Until then there is a mingling of the faithful and the pretenders. This is the parable of inclusiveness. How might these parables speak to the openness of our front door?

After years of experimentation and reflection — and membership protocols that tended to err on the side of inclusiveness — our staff came to the conclusion that our membership process could and should be far more than a perfunctory series of classes. We've elected to challenge our inquirers to a seven-week series of interactions with staff members, lay leaders, and other inquirers that clearly communicates the mission of our church and *actually initiates* the behaviors that are consistent with being a disciple of Jesus. This ministry consists of four main features.

First, we explore with integrity our inquirers' commitment to Christ. Membership in a PC(USA) congregation is predicated on a simple three-word confession: "Christ is Lord." What is our responsibility in discerning the authenticity of the one who speaks? I am a reasonably observant person. It's not hard to read the face of the bored or resistant husband in the Inquirers Class whose expression fairly shouts, "I'm here because *she* wants me to do this. Now let's get this over with."

We have begun to include in our membership process a talk on the dangers of spiritual perjury. As Jesus put it, by our own words we will be acquitted and by the public statements we make we will be condemned. We clearly teach that it does not matter *what* path we have followed to faith, or precisely *when* we came to faith, but it is crucial that we *do now stand in faith* before God. We present the good news of Jesus and insist that the salvation offered in the Bible requires a response of the whole person. Those who have unanswered questions, we invite to meet with a staff person. During almost every class, a discerning leader identifies an inquirer who needs further reflection, more time or more information to make a decision. Honest discussion over a lunch follows. Occasionally we recommend that an inquirer postpone joining until he or she has come to a threshold of spiritual clarity. We do our best to prevent members from crossing their fingers during a public confession.

Second, we present and carefully analyze the mission, vision, and values of the congregation. We demonstrate how the six marks of a disciple are the behaviors that alone are able to move a mission statement (*Growing and serving together in Christ so that all may know his love*) from the front of the Sunday bulletin to one's calendar, purse, and thought life.

Growing up in his native India, author Ravi Zacharias used to participate in a strange event called the slow cycling race during a community sports day. The goal of the race was not to take off as soon as the gun sounded, but to move as slowly as possible. In fact, it was best if you could remain standing still on your bicycle, your feet not touching the ground. The goal of the race was to come in last. Some competitors were so adept at staying stationary that the distance of the race was only a few yards.

Imagine a visiting cycling champion from another country standing there before the gun sounds. He sees everyone get on his bike and he thinks, "I wish I could be in this race and teach these beginners a few things about cycling." If he's offered the opportunity, imagine his astonishment when at the sound of the gun he speeds off and breaks through the tape first, only to look back and see the rest of the cyclists still at the starting line trying to balance their motionless bikes. Imagine his astonishment when he discovers that he has finished *last* even though he crossed the line *first*.

It pays to know the purpose of a race before we try to win it. It pays to know the purpose of involvement in the body of Christ before we speed off, assuming we're winning, when in fact we can't even state the reason that Christ has called us to be part of his body. We desire the new member entering our congregation to have a full awareness and a growing commitment to our mission and values . . . and an idea of what it would look like to live them out.

In that regard, third, every inquirer completes a spiritual gift instrument designed especially for our congregation that tests for twenty divine enablements. One of the sessions of the new member process at our church is reserved for teaching about the gifts and call the Spirit bestows on every believer. By appointment at a later time, every inquirer spends up to an hour with a member of the Ambassadors, a team of "involvement interviewers" who have a keen awareness of the seventy-five or so ministries of our church. The interviewer assesses the background, interests, experiences, gifts, concerns, and dreams of the new member and works to make appropriate "ministry matches," contacting ministry leaders on behalf of the inquirer, and staying in touch with these new members for up to six months to help them over the rough spots of assimilation.

We have discovered that members new and old regularly need a refresher course on these matters, so they are highlighted annually from the pulpit. One Sunday in September is set aside for a morning-long Ministry Fair that allows publicity for the ministries, opportunities to interact with team leaders, and recruitment of volunteers. Every year we revise and update a strategic booklet, the *Zionsville Presbyterian Church Guidebook,* which includes printed descriptions of ministries and team leader phone numbers for every functioning group and ministry in the church. Several Sundays a month I invite members and guests to pick up a *Guidebook* at our welcome center and consider their next step of involvement in the kingdom.

Fourth, we have added homework to our inquirers process. All new members write out and submit (for discussion with a staff person) a personal plan for spiritual growth, specifying how they intend to build the values of discipleship into their lives. Without an action plan we don't get very far. This personalized document is ideally the doorway to moving into a small group, involvement in a cursillo retreat experience, Sunday or midweek classes, mission endeavors, and an ongoing commitment to spiritual disciplines.

I've been watching birds off and on for about thirty years. It's an interesting hobby because birds are constantly in motion, and you can't always see what you'd like. Early on I thought the key achievement in bird-watching was to tally up a huge life list of the birds I had seen. I kept adding to my list by going on hikes with skilled guides. They could see and hear things I could never pick up. I remember being on a hike when one of my guides said, "Now up in that tree there's a Cerulean Warbler." Cerulean Warblers are tiny birds, turquoise blue, with magically beautiful voices. I looked and I looked. I could hear it, but I couldn't see it. But my guide had spotted it, and I was with the guide, so I marked it down. At the time it was gratifying to put another check on my life list, but today I feel differently. Today I want to see a Cerulean Warbler for myself.

What is my deepest wish for those entering our congregation? It is that when it comes to Jesus Christ, they will insist on *seeing him for themselves* — never being satisfied with somebody else's prayers, somebody else's service, somebody else's experience of the power and presence of God. May there be no spiritual hitch-hikers in the church, but only those who with integrity can say that Christ is Lord, and *their* Lord, indeed.

QUESTIONS FOR REFLECTION AND DISCUSSION

1. How are persons initiated into your church (taken into membership)? How does your procedure relate to those used in "the cultural church"?
2. How can Jesus' way of initiating new persons into his community inform your own process?
3. What difference does the cultural situation in the United States make in our forms of initiating persons into the church?
4. What can you learn from other traditions of initiation? From pastor McDonald's method? What would be the values to your church of a carefully conceived and developed method of initiation?

CHAPTER FOUR

Prayer in the Spirit

N O ACT COMES nearer to describing the Church in the Spirit than prayer. Prayer is the life breath of the church; it is the natural posture of the people of God; it is the means of healing and the source of empowerment. The Church in the Spirit, therefore, will be grounded in the practice of prayer. To discover material for imagining the church that believes in prayer and lives prayer, we will look at the prayer life of Jesus which also inspired the early church. These two sources will provide appropriate images for imagining a church that not only grounds its life and mission in prayer but depends on this communion with God for guidance, nurture, and empowerment for ministry.

Prayer in the Cultural Church

Consider the role of prayer in the typical mainline congregation. In too many instances both pastors and members have lost faith in prayer as little more than autosuggestion. The rational views of the Enlightenment and the ensuing religious skepticism have reduced prayer to an exercise in remembering.

Prayer is what pastors and people do when they have run out of options.

Prayer receives token recognition at worship services, funerals, weddings, and in hospital rooms. These are the expected places for prayer, and professional praying finds expression in all these situations.

Some congregations begin their official meetings with prayer, but not all remember this simple gesture of gratitude and surrender.

Along with the church's shallow use of prayer, every congregation has a few persons who believe in the living presence of Christ and the efficacy of believing prayer. These persons generally have a disciplined approach to prayer, a way of opening themselves to God, a way of listening, and sources of spiritual encouragement. And it may well be their faithfulness that keeps their particular congregation alive.

If prayer gives life to the church and constitutes the core of ministry, why do ministers have such a hard time praying?

And why are they embarrassed to pray in the presence of another minister? Is it that they know the other minister recognizes their professionalism?

Foundational Convictions of a Praying Church

The Church in the Spirit, grounded in the Cosmic Christ, has its foundation in Jesus of Nazareth who is the norm of the church's life and the model of its prayer. The Cosmic Christ is the medium, conduit, and agent of the Spirit. He is the Spirit of the church; therefore, these convictions drive the praying church:

- The Church in the Spirit will be motivated by the conviction that the personal presence of Christ creates and sustains it.
- The Church in the Spirit knows that communion with Christ nourishes, sustains, and energizes it. Therefore, the Church in the Spirit will be a community of profound prayer.
- The prayer of the Church in the Spirit will be informed and driven by the conviction of an unseen but real world of the Spirit. This is not a second world behind the visible world but the energy, presence, spirit, and power that penetrate the material

61

world and are accessible to all persons but discerned only by people of faith. Within and beyond the material world this community of faith experiences the Christ dimension, in which prayer, faith, and love count as fundamental realities.

- The Church in the Spirit has an enormous capacity to engage the transcendent world, be informed and empowered by this spiritual dimension of existence, and to demonstrate the reality of the kingdom in tangible actions of compassion and justice.

Prayer in the Life and Ministry of Jesus

If we are to imagine the church in the image of Christ, it is imperative that we look at the prayer life of Jesus as one aspect of the model. Even a cursory review of his prayer life indicates that he prayed during his days in the desert, before he chose his disciples, after he had performed the feeding miracle, and on the mountain before facing his great test in Jerusalem. He taught his disciples to pray and he struggled in prayer before he was betrayed, tried, and crucified. Prayer punctuated his whole life and ministry and offers the church a model for its life.

After the baptism Jesus, full of the Spirit, was led into the wilderness to be tempted. Can you imagine those days he spent alone, and can you imagine fasting as anything but continuous prayer to God? Luke reports his wilderness experience briefly:

> Jesus, full of the Holy Spirit, returned from the Jordan and was led by the Spirit in the wilderness, where for forty days he was tempted by the devil. He ate nothing at all during those days, and when they were over, he was famished. (Luke 4:1-2)

Before calling his disciples, training them, and sending them forth as apostles, Jesus spent a whole night in prayer. Perhaps prayer was essential for his discernment; it cleared his mind and gave him insight into the persons whom he should choose to carry on his ministry. Again, Luke gives us a thumbnail sketch:

Now during those days he went out to the mountain to pray; and he spent the night in prayer to God. And when day came, he called his disciples and chose twelve of them, whom he also named apostles. (Luke 6:12-13)

After Jesus had fed the multitude he prayed, modeling how after a special manifestation of the Spirit, those who are used by God are vulnerable to temptation and despair. To combat the despair Jesus spent hours alone in prayer. Prayer not only protected him from the Evil One, but prepared him for the next disclosure of himself to the disciples.

And after he had dismissed the crowds, he went up the mountain by himself to pray. When evening came, he was there alone, but by this time the boat, battered by the waves, was far from the land, for the wind was against them. And early in the morning he came walking toward them on the sea. But when the disciples saw him walking on the sea, they were terrified, saying, "It is a ghost!" And they cried out in fear. But immediately Jesus spoke to them and said, "Take heart, it is I; do not be afraid." Peter answered him, "Lord, if it is you, command me to come to you on the water." He said, "Come." So Peter got out of the boat, started walking on the water, and came toward Jesus. But when he noticed the strong wind, he became frightened, and beginning to sink, he cried out, "Lord, save me!" Jesus immediately reached out his hand and caught him, saying to him, "You of little faith, why did you doubt?" When they got into the boat, the wind ceased. (Matt. 14:23-32)

Jesus' dependence on prayer during his ministry did not go unnoticed by his disciples. Knowing that John the Baptist had instructed his followers in prayer, Jesus' disciples said to him, "Lord, teach us to pray as John taught his disciples." This request according to Luke gave occasion for Jesus to offer his disciples the prayer that is said most often, the Lord's Prayer, or more precisely, the disciple's prayer.

He was praying in a certain place, and after he had finished, one of his disciples said to him, "Lord, teach us to pray, as John taught his disciples." He said to them, "When you pray, say: Father, hallowed be your name. Your kingdom come. Give us each day our daily bread. And forgive us our sins, for we ourselves forgive everyone indebted to us. And do not bring us to the time of trial." (Luke 11:1-4)

When Jesus knew that he would soon face death, he prepared his disciples to face their grief through prayer. He went up on a mountain to pray and took with him Peter, James, and John. While he prayed, his garments glistened with light, a voice spoke, and the disciples were overwhelmed with the revelation. Later they understood the connection between prayer and the revelation of the Spirit and the empowerment of Jesus for the suffering that lay before him.

Now about eight days after these sayings Jesus took with him Peter and John and James, and went up on the mountain to pray. And while he was praying, the appearance of his face changed, and his clothes became dazzling white. Suddenly they saw two men, Moses and Elijah, talking to him. They appeared in glory and were speaking of his departure, which he was about to accomplish at Jerusalem. Now Peter and his companions were weighed down with sleep; but since they had stayed awake, they saw his glory and the two men who stood with him. (Luke 9:28-32)

When Jesus faced the greatest trial of his life, he prayed. He knew the end was near. The supper had ended; Judas had been dismissed. Then Jesus invited the disciples to the Mount of Olives to join him in prayer. He struggled with God, asking that God take away the cup of pain and suffering, but the cup was not removed. And Jesus concluded his prayer with the ultimate prayer for him and for us all, "Not my will but yours be done."

He came out and went, as was his custom, to the Mount of Olives; and the disciples followed him. When he reached the place, he said to them, "Pray that you may not come into the time of trial." Then he withdrew from them about a stone's throw, knelt down, and prayed, "Father, if you are willing, remove this cup from me; yet, not my will but yours be done." Then an angel from heaven appeared to him and gave him strength. In his anguish he prayed more earnestly, and his sweat became like great drops of blood falling down on the ground. When he got up from prayer, he came to the disciples and found them sleeping because of grief, and he said to them, "Why are you sleeping? Get up and pray that you may not come into the time of trial." (Luke 22:39-46)

Imagining a Praying Church

If the life and ministry of Jesus provide a paradigm for the church, his prayer life provides multiple symbols for picturing the church at prayer. The examples cited in the ministry of Jesus illustrate how the church can embrace prayer in its corporate life as Jesus prayed in his life and ministry.

It is important for us to keep in mind that the specifics of Jesus' practice of prayer illustrate but do not limit the modes of our prayer. Today's church does not copy the example of Jesus in the first century but uses the content and form of his prayer to imagine the church's practice of prayer in the twenty first century. To continue this prayer through his body on earth, the Jesus of history has been liberated by the resurrection and the ascension to be the ever-present Christ praying through his church now. Because he is Lord of the church, he may teach us ways of prayer in our communal life which are only foreshadowed in the biblical witness.

How do we today imagine the church as a corporate expression of Christ in its prayer? Take the wilderness experience as a beginning. The Spirit led Christ into the wilderness for testing and it became the place of encounter with Evil as well as a place of solitude and prayer.

This experience of Jesus, at the dawn of his ministry, suggests that the church may on occasion find itself in the wilderness, perhaps for both testing and instruction. In the wilderness, distractions fade away and the community in its solitude will come to greater clarity of purpose. Clarity leads to unity and empowerment.

A wilderness in corporate form may be the decline in membership, the loss of status in the culture, or the failure of a project. In either of these threatening experiences, the church may feel marginalized or it may question its motives. These periods of dryness in congregational life can be ignored or hidden, but taken as a wilderness testing, they can drive the church to serious prayer.

Or a wilderness for the congregation may take the form of an annual retreat in which the leaders take three or four days to pray about the church's ministry. The question for those days would be "What are you calling us to be and do in your name?" Marked with silence, these days of prayer, worship, and solitude become the chamber for discernment.

And, as Jesus returned in the power of the Spirit to minister in Galilee, the leadership will return with a deep sense of call and empowerment for ministry in our world.

Jesus spent the night in prayer before calling his disciples. The connection between his prayer for discernment and ours does not present us with a wide gulf to span. How much difference would it make if our choices of leaders grew out of prayer and discernment? I am convinced that Jesus not only prayed about the selection of the disciples but that he continued to pray for them in their ministry. Even now he prays for them that they may be empowered by the Spirit.

Jesus' extended period of prayer after the feeding miracle suggests that the church should respond to successful ventures with prayer. Most churches think about prayer before a stewardship campaign or a building program or a mission conference. Often, someone will suggest that God be given praise for the success of the effort, but the fervor of thanksgiving rarely equals the urgency of our petition for help. An extended time of thanksgiving provides the proper closure for God's blessing and it defends the church against pride and sloth.

Jesus' taking three disciples up the mountain to pray might suggest that the pastor of a congregation needs two or three persons to share the burden of leadership. What pastor does not need a few close friends with whom to share personal concerns, needs, and dreams? Peter, James, and John seem to have had that kind of relationship with Jesus. This incident may also suggest the importance of prayer in the face of a crisis — prayer before it comes, not after it has arisen.

Jesus' disciples asked him to instruct them in prayer. If we aim for prayer to penetrate a congregation, members must be taught to pray. The Spirit teaches us to pray and all the baptized receive the Spirit. The example of the congregation living a disciplined life of prayer, may be the best instruction members receive. For prayer to be mature and grounded, however, the church needs to take responsibility for teaching all its members to pray. Classes on prayer, sermons on prayer, prayer retreats, mentors, and spiritual guides all offer ways that a church can be taught to pray. The church fulfills its role as a corporate expression of Christ when it teaches persons to pray.

If the church prays as Jesus did in the garden, in a crisis it will not think first of a lawsuit, of judging others, or of alienating itself from the offender. If there comes a time when persecution is aimed at the church in the West, it will no doubt turn to prayer. The praying church will seek the will of God before it reacts to a crisis.

These illustrations provide simple beginning points for imagining the church as the corporate Christ who prays about every aspect of its life and witness to the world. If the church incarnates the life of Christ in each age, how can it fail to make prayer the central focus of its life and ministry?

Imagining the Church at Prayer

Various forms of prayer provide the means to engage and transact with this Other Side of Reality of which we, at best, are only dimly aware. To fully develop the life of prayer in the congregation, we might consider these challenges: to speak with Jesus as naturally as he spoke with the Father; or to listen to the voice of God as Jesus listened to that voice in the desert; to read the texts as Jesus read from the books of Moses and the Psalms; to discern the presence in everyday life as Jesus welcomed the Father's presence in the persons to whom he ministered; or to contemplate the material of earth in the light of eternity; and engage the Sacred Silence where spirit meets Spirit.

Imagine a congregation in which persons enter the place of worship with a prayer on their lips. Quiet before God, each would be an open channel for the Spirit. As these persons participate in the liturgy they will sense the overpowering presence of the Holy One in their midst.

How might the church learn to listen for God? Worship, of course, can be laced with silence as persons center themselves in the presence. But consider also how listening in silence at the beginning of meetings can become a form of prayer and a prelude to discernment for a praying church.

Reading scripture alone and in groups offers yet another way of prayer. For too many years reading scripture has been experienced as a cognitive enterprise rather than an opportunity to listen for God. Listening for God in scripture provides yet another way to pray.

When the whole congregation begins to look for God in the events of the day, it will fire the corporate imagination. After a week living in the presence of the living God, the people will come together with a new vision, and a passion to participate in kingdom ministry. For them, action becomes prayer and prayer becomes action in the world.

This practice of looking for God in the ordinary leads to a profound sense of the Holy in all of life. Soon the church learns to contemplate everything — words, feelings, relationships, and the art of nature — against the backdrop of eternity.

All these ways of corporate and personal prayer lead into the sacred silence of God. How powerful, how transformative will the church become when it reclaims this central practice of its life, prayer!

A Corroborative Witness

The ultimate fool attempts to lead the establishment of God's work without being in significant conversation with God. Who would dare participate in a ministry without a bedrock foundation of prayer?

Well, that would be me. During the first decade of my involvement at the Zionsville Church I reasoned that there were other arrows in my quiver. Things were going well. The congregation was growing. Ministries were proliferating. Whenever I would enter a period of silence and reflection, however, the reality of my arrogance would hit me like a sledgehammer: *I was leaving God out of a ministry that was being offered in God's name.*

It wasn't hard to imagine Jesus' words at the end of the Sermon on the Mount being spoken to me: "Many will say to me on that day, 'Lord, Lord, didn't we establish a whale of a new church in your name? Didn't we blow away everybody's numerical projections?' Then I will tell them plainly, 'I never knew you. Away from me, you evildoers!'" (Matt. 7:22, 23 paraphrased). *I never knew you.* Ministry's bottom line is not the number of faces in the pictorial directory but whether any have been ushered into intimacy with God.

The telltale marks of a prayer-impoverished leadership style were evident in every corner of my life. I found myself afflicted by the need to push myself and to push others, when regular quiet times would undoubtedly have connected me with Jesus' voice in Mark 6:31: "Come with me by yourselves to a quiet place and get some rest." In his book *Into Thin Air,* Jon Krakauer recounts the deaths in 1996 of eight skilled climbers who were attempting to reach the crest of Mt. Everest. Some died because of the intoxication of "summit fever," the obsession to continue striving for irrational goals, no matter what, even in the midst of dangerous circumstances — long after one's physical and emotional energies are spent. Spiritual summit fever regularly seduced me into working longer and harder on particular projects — sometimes months after the Spirit of God had moved on to a new work. I was frankly too busy to listen for the Spirit's voice.

My self-dependence was also on display when lay people approached me and expressed the desire to pray for my ministry, my health, my family, and my life with God. I tended to deflect such requests with false modesty. "What a nice thing to ask! But why don't you pray about something that *really* matters?" I attempted to redirect their prayers to vague global concerns. Their surprise and disappointment should have alerted me to what I know much better today: treating the requests of potential prayer partners as of little value simply evidences ignorance of prayer's real power.

Some of the wonderful lay people of our church, however, did not abandon their attempts to pray for me. They were growing in their own experience of prayer and they were determined to become supportive of their pastor. They wrote encouraging notes to me that mentioned their commitment to prayer. They quizzed me when we met in the grocery store, searching for details about the needs of my family. They were irrepressible!

About 1993 a small cadre of these praying individuals began to arrive on our church property before anyone else on Sunday mornings. They walked all over our parking lot, hiked along the perimeter of our property, stepped into each classroom, and quietly moved among the chairs in our worship area — all the while praying for the opening of the hearts and minds of all who would be on site that Sunday. Early one January morning as I drove into our parking lot I remember shivering in the predawn darkness, nursing my car slowly over snow and ice. There in the gloom were two members of the prayer team, bundled up and carefully skirting patches of ice, walking along the border of our property. "These people must be on prayer steroids," I concluded.

About that time things began to change at Zionsville Presbyterian Church. I cannot quantify the changes precisely. I can only say that those leading and participating in our Sunday morning gatherings became more profoundly aware of the presence of God. The thermostat of our spiritual warmth had been adjusted upward. I know that my heart began to thaw, too. I began to welcome, then to eagerly anticipate, the brief time before our first service when the prayer team would come into the office, join hands with the worship leaders, and hold up the totality of the morning's events before God.

Who would dare to attempt ministry without a bedrock foundation of prayer? I confess that I shudder at the ignorance and faithlessness of my first fifteen years as a pastor. Today the growth and diversification of the prayer life of our congregation has at last become a notable feature. We have found that increasing numbers of adults and youth are drawn into deeper prayer lives as (1) prayer is publicly spotlighted by leaders as a non-negotiable element of a healthy life before God; (2) those who have gone a few steps further in this adventure choose to exercise the "come with me" principle, mentoring others quietly over many months; (3) avid readers in the congregation discover — and pass along to others — the treasures of the classical prayer literature produced by the cloud of witnesses of earlier Christian history; and, most importantly, (4) individuals actually *experience* for themselves what it's like to be intimately connected with God. Perfunctory prayers before meals and meetings can never be the same after that.

Our exploration and experimentation with corporate prayer has led to the establishment of new ministries. Each Sunday, three different teams of *chapel counselors* (each supporting a different worship service) plant members in the chapel down the corridor from our main worship space. These individuals, together or on their own, spend the entire worship hour in prayer and reflection, asking the Spirit to work powerfully in the hearts of those who are worshiping. They are thus uniquely prepared to meet those who respond to our service-concluding invitation to spend more time with God in the chapel. Every few months these teams also gather for prayer with each other, and also for celebration, assessment, and training to better extend God's grace to those who come with specific needs.

Several lay people who were motivated to spend meaningful time with God but were disturbed by their own inconsistency in that venture began to rely on personal *prayer calendars*. They committed each day of the week to a series of specific requests, in the categories of God's nature, God's direction over church, family, and personal life, and global issues. Thursday's prayers, for example, might include regular expressions of thanks for the Holy Spirit's guidance, intercession for the music ministry of our church, and petition for spiritual awakening in Europe. For those who are determined to carve out regular times of communication with God, this pattern works. It was no surprise that other church members began to say, "Would you show me how you drew up that calendar of yours?" Dozens of members and friends of the church have now undertaken this discipline.

Historically, our corporate prayer muscles were most atrophied at the beginning of *elders' meetings*. Faced with another three-hour siege of agenda items, I figured that these bright "spiritual leaders" would want to dive right in to business. So that's the behavior I modeled. Our time of opening prayer rarely exceeded the length of the treasurer's report stating our current cash position.

Once again, our awakening to prayer came about through lay leaders who initiated a new emphasis at our "business" meetings. During a retreat one of the elders spoke for the whole group. "We come to meetings right from work, or a rushed dinner, or an exhausting day chasing kids. In no way are we prepared to hear what God is saying to the church. We need to begin with an extended period of silence, reflection, and prayer." I suggested thirty minutes. They voted forty-five instead. Our meetings now begin with a scripture reading and a stated prayer theme for the evening — generally one that has direct correlation to issues that will be on the table. We customarily break into groups of three or four. Occasionally members of the group walk to a part of the building that reflects an aspect of our ministry that weighs on their heart — the youth room, for example, or the office, or the information booth where Sunday morning guests first arrive. Each elder in turn offers prayer that God would empower and direct that field of ministry.

In addition to several groups that receive and pray for congregational prayer requests, a widening circle gathers every other Tuesday evening to ask God for a deeper movement of the Spirit in Zionsville. Small groups go about the quiet but life-giving business of modeling a sustained conversation with God. Several key leaders forge ahead with their dream of establishing around-the-clock prayer coverage for our church and its members by inviting individuals to "adopt" a half-hour segment of prayer every week (say, Friday from 3:30 to 4:00 P.M.).

With the recent emphasis on prayer motion and prayer technique within our church, it's been more urgent than ever to remember that *God is a real person who is always speaking*. That alone is why prayer makes a difference. Our listening is a higher priority than our verbalizing. One wise leader counsels, "Just show up and shut up." In prayer our church is gradually discovering the astonishing truth that we already have everything we seek and everything we need. Even this pastor who's been addicted to summit fever is beginning to learn that you don't need to climb ministry mountains to obtain what God gives for free.

QUESTIONS FOR REFLECTION AND DISCUSSION

1. How would you describe the corporate prayer life of your congregation?
2. Reflect on the foundational convictions held by a Church in the Spirit. Which of these seem important to you? Which convictions influence your life and the life of your congregation?
3. How is Jesus' life of prayer a paradigm for the congregation? Why should it be?
4. What part of Pastor McDonald's witness inspires you to emphasize prayer in your congregation?

CHAPTER FIVE

Discerning a Church's Mission in the Spirit

A CHURCH THAT DISCERNS its mission, in contrast with the church that plans a program, will become one of the marks of the Church in the Spirit. In its discernment of mission this congregation will have a central focus, experience creativity and joy, and find energy through the Spirit to perform its tasks. Discernment of call will force the church to deal directly with the risen Lord. This intimate transaction with Christ will occur as the church opens itself to his living presence in its midst. In this encounter it receives both a disclosure and empowerment to carry out the mission.

Discernment of mission may not, perhaps, issue in vast changes in the final action the congregation undertakes, but the practice of discernment will vastly change how the church arrives at its vision and carries out its ministry. The task of discernment proceeds with the conviction that the church has been created to do the will of God, not its own will. It also believes that God can disclose the divine will to human beings in a form they can understand and appropriate. These convictions about the nature of mission also make dealing directly with God unavoidable. Consider these questions about your present way of defining your work:

- How does your congregation decide on its mission?
- How does God engage the leadership?
- How are visions for ministry confirmed?
- What are the criteria for decision making?

Imagine a typical planning session in the cultural church. Too often it begins with the wrong questions: What did we do last year? Should we do the same this year? What was the budget previously? Can we cut it 20 percent this year? What will get more people involved in the work? Should we first serve our own members and then the needs of others?

These questions ignore three central aspects of mission. First, God's will for the particular congregation is never acknowledged. The needs of a person outside the church have no way of getting into the planning. And, the gifts and sense of call of the members do not receive consideration. This line of questioning leads to a plan describing what we wish to do for God. And, the whole plan can be developed and executed without ever dealing directly with God in any conscious, intentional way. Our present way of initiating mission has maintained the cultural church, but the time has come for us to scuttle it in favor of a model that places our dependence squarely upon God.

Most cultural churches have embraced a management model of ministry, a model that does not seriously consider God's call to the church. This alien model begins with our thoughts, feelings, and needs, and depends on human agency to achieve goals. As a consequence, the church seldom mentions the name of God or seeks God's counsel. I long for the church to shift from this management model to a discernment model that demands we face God's will and call. Discernment changes the question from, "What do we want to do for God?" to "What is God calling us to be and do?" When this shift takes place, the congregation must listen for God to speak and discern together the mind of God.

Discernment demands seriousness about God and God's will. There can be no rehearsal or practice sessions in discernment. Planning allows for tests and rehearsals, but not so with discernment. To inquire about God's will hinges on a readiness to do it. God does not reveal the divine will for us to debate or evaluate. What God wills, we are to do! Discernment implies commitment.

The Mission

The mission of the church is to re-present Jesus Christ to the world in an incarnate, communal form. This task begins with the consciousness of Christ as the living foundation for the church's life. The presence is clothed with the baptized members. The re-presentation of Christ manifests itself in concrete acts of ministry through a particular congregation that has heard his call.

The mission of the church is not to . . .

- fulfill its own wishes.
- proclaim the gospel according to the world's tastes and preferences.
- gain more members or increase its prominence in the community.
- impress those who either observe or participate in the life of the church.

All these distortions of mission occur when the church concerns itself with a goal other than the will of God.

The determining issue in mission rests upon the call of Christ. What is Jesus Christ calling a particular congregation to be and do, in this place, at this time? This disclosure of Christ's comes to a congregation through the Spirit. The Spirit calls, and when the church hears and responds, Christ embodies himself in each particular ministry. Do you not find it amazing, a small group of believers becomes his body doing ministry? Mission grounds the congregation in Christ, and his call is mediated through the Spirit in a personal, responsible manner. Affirming Christ as the initiator of mission relates every act of the church to him so that the church does indeed become the visible, tangible presence of Christ in the world.

Instruments for Discerning God's Call

Imagine that your congregation has chosen to take seriously its mission to re-present Christ. How does he make known his call to the leadership and the congregation? I believe that Christ calls through his Word, through the pain of suffering people, through his own model of service, and through the gifts of persons in his body. Consider how you may engage each of these sources to discern your mission.

The text of scripture. The primary and normative instrument of call is the text of scripture. This Word of God mediates the truth of God and the will of God to the church. The biblical text defines the basis of mission in Christ (the why of mission); the expression of mission (the how of mission); it transforms our imagination so that acts of compassion and obedience show us the kingdom (the purpose of mission). These claims for scripture justify making it normative for mission. The living Christ, who is the church's life, guides his church through the text of scripture as he once guided his disciples through verbal directives.

The context of the church. Mission always occurs in a particular place. Context points to the social, political, and geographic situation in which a particular congregation finds itself. While the scriptures inspire and drive mission, the context informs the content, method, and aim of mission. The content of the mission derives from the form of Christ in our situation of ministry. We ask, "How can our actions manifest Christ in this context?" Making Christ visible is always the operative norm.

The context determines the method of ministry. We would hardly minister to business leaders in the same way we would minister to residents at a retirement home. Yet, the aim of mission remains constant — to manifest Jesus Christ.

Perhaps these questions will help clarify our mission perspective: To whom do we minister? What are their needs? What can be done by the grace of God? What are the options for achieving the mission? In what way will our actions manifest the Christ we know in scripture and in the living fellowship of the community? The physical form of Christ may appear in a variety of shapes, usually determined by the need.

Since the person of Christ defines the norm of our mission, we will find ourselves asking of each mission opportunity, "What aspect of the person of Christ applies to this need? Is the need for healing, food, or freedom from oppression?" The congregation discerns how Christ wills to express himself through this particular body in response to specific needs. Obviously, the church makes an imaginative leap from Jesus Christ of the first century to the living Christ in the fellowship of believers today. This imaginative leap from Christ in us to Christ meeting human need through us invites persistent discernment. In no other way does the church witness so effectively to Christ as through these acts of compassion.

Gifts of the people of God. The substance of mission will be defined in part by the gifts and resources of a particular congregation. The gifts inherent in a particular church define the dynamic inner working of ministry. The availability of persons, the gifts of the Spirit to the congregation, and the financial resources in the congregation give the mission substance. Without persons, gifts of the Spirit, and financial resources, how could mission occur? Remember! Christ does not call a congregation to do what he has not given it gifts to do.

The revealing work of the Spirit. The Spirit of Christ moves upon the text, in the context, to call forth the gifts of the people to manifest the kingdom. This call, through the work of the Spirit, unites the living Christ with human need in a particular place. This initial connection between the living presence of Christ and the mission of a congregation requires creative imagination. For example, migrant Mexican workers move into a community, presenting numerous opportunities for ministry. Many do not speak English, others have difficulty with the law; some feel a need to worship but there is no place for them. All these needs call for ministry. Responding to any of them would be consistent with the ministry of Jesus and the text of scripture. But a congregation may have gifts and resources to respond to one need and not to another. Certain members of the congregation may have gifts to help with the language problem, but no knowledge of legal problems. When a number of demands present themselves, the Holy Spirit shows a congregation what to do. The Spirit reveals the mind of Christ through the minds, hearts, and gifts of the people. Whatever the mission, the action arises from Christ, is empowered by Christ, and manifests Christ.

Has writing this book been a call to ministry, inspired by the Spirit? I visit congregations that seem spiritually dead or dying, and their ineffectiveness evokes enormous pain in me. Other congregations are vital, active, and effective in mission. I wonder if the Holy Spirit has worked in my mind, stirring my imagination to envision a new way of being the church, a new way of thinking about ministry and mission. I have wondered if this experience, in some remote way, may be an instance of the revealing work of the Spirit through an encounter with the church's need and the gifts and resources that I bring to the issue.

The providential manner in which the thoughts in this book came into print also makes me wonder if God may have been involved. The Director of Advanced Studies asked me to teach a summer course to doctoral students. In the following week, the basic outline of what I have written emerged from my mind, one idea after another. Increasingly, these ideas began to shape my teaching and leadership in the church. Perhaps what you do with the suggestions in these chapters will become part of the discernment of whether the idea was of God.

The Criteria of Discernment

Without discernment none of us can fulfill the mission of Christ in the world. Our greatest fear seems always to be that we will mistake our own subconscious yearnings for the voice of Christ. Through the long history of the church, God's people have dealt with this question, and have forged dependable principles that help us with our discernment.

The process of discernment has both subjective and objective criteria. The *external* criteria of discernment include:

- The person and work of Jesus Christ as revealed in the New Testament.
- The writings of the apostles.
- The tradition of the church, the long memory that holds the ways in which discernment has taken place.

• The practice of a modified consensus in the body of Christ.
• The principle of correspondence, that is, the unity of the inward and outward criteria of discernment. Correspondence occurs when the gifts, persons, and resources of the community match the need, opportunity, and issues in the context.

These objective aspects of a call provide external norms of discernment. The internal norms of discernment include criteria of a personal, subjective nature. These internal norms include clarity, persistence, conviction, and peace. Consider these questions that test the ministry to which you may feel called:

• Is there *clarity* about the need and the manner of response?
• Does the call to this mission *persist* over a period of time?
• Is there a shared *conviction* that God is calling us to this action?
• When we contemplate this action in the name of Christ, do we have *peace?*

Data collected through asking these questions hinge on crucial internal norms for the church's discernment of Christ. In the illustration of the migrant workers, for example, perhaps one person brings to the church a conviction that the church should provide classes in English. When the governing body of the church decides, it reviews all the data. The leaders turn to God in prayer, opening themselves to the guidance of the Spirit. Opportunity is given for a full, open discussion of the insights that came in the prayer.

Those seeking discernment quickly recognize that this ministry accords with the Spirit of Christ; it is consistent with the teaching of the New Testament and the tradition of the church; members of the congregation have begun to respond to the call of Christ. With respect to the internal aspects of discernment, the leaders are clear, the call persists in their hearts, and there is a conviction that they should undertake this mission to meet the needs of the workers. Only the Spirit, however, determines whether this ministry re-presents Christ.

Discernment in this situation is simple, but other issues of discernment carry heavier emotional freight and will not be resolved so quickly or easily. For example, the ordination of gay or lesbian persons will certainly evoke deeper and more seriously conflicting emotions that challenge the process. Discernment always seeks clarity about the voice of God, and frequently must work through deeply entrenched attitudes and feelings. Discerning God's voice will take longer, but it is the biblical way for a faithful church to open the door into the future.

Stages of Discernment

As we begin practicing discernment in our congregations, we should not expect discernment to be instantaneous and immediate. Generally, a confident discernment process evolves over a period of time. During the waiting period, the community tests its hunches, then shapes and reshapes its sense of call. In this process of discernment the community generally passes through stages of awareness, interest, naming the call, being sent in mission, and obedience.

Awareness. A need may exist long before anyone notices it. When the Spirit awakens the consciousness of a member or a group of members to a particular need or opportunity, they attend the call. Like Moses, whose attention was grasped by the burning bush, these persons can no longer ignore the pain or hunger of persons. The "burning bush quality" awakens persons to the opportunity for ministry.

Interest. The situation that comes into our awareness may awaken a positive interest that draws the person to the need, or it may send out negative vibrations that frighten the would-be missionary. A mark of the Spirit's presence seems to be the birth of passion to respond to the call. John's testimony to Jesus, for example, awakened an interest in a few of his disciples, and they followed Jesus to his place of abode and talked with him for several hours.

Naming. At the outset the discernment may be unclear, composed of awareness and interest, but the course of action lacks clear definition. The bush that burned and burned without being consumed got Moses' attention, but he did not know the meaning of the awesome event. His awakened interest caused him to turn aside and he heard a voice speaking to him. At that point he could name the experience be-

81

cause the occurrence had gone beyond mere awareness and interest. The God of his fathers was speaking through the bush but Moses had not yet received the call. In the process of discernment we are often convinced that God is speaking to us, but we do not know what to do.

Being sent. Mature discernment calls for action; it tells us what we are to do. If the Lord reveals himself to you or to your community it is for a purpose, to participate specifically in the plan of God for persons and for the world. God does not give information to amuse us or to satisfy our curiosity but to help us act in accord with his purpose.

First steps of obedience. Final discernment comes through obedience. Most of us would like to have a crystal ball that reveals the future, showing us where our obedience will lead. Yet we must act in faith based on our discernment of obedience, without proof. When we obey, the landscape sometimes shifts and the strategy and response change with it. Our insights into God's will do not predict the future or make known the challenges before us, yet we are always accompanied by the promise of presence as the journey unfolds.

These stages of discernment may occur in the sequence noted or they may not. Sometimes all these stages seem to occur simultaneously. Whatever the process of discernment, it must be tested by the criteria and confirmed by the community.

Testing discernment in a community. Generally the subject for discernment grasps an individual first. A person feels a hunger, discovers an opportunity, or encounters human pain, and these experiences provide data for discernment. Before bringing this matter to the governing body of the church, the member should . . .

- Test the discernment with another trusted disciple.
- Share his or her understanding with a larger group of persons and profit from their response.
- Issue a call to see if others feel called to share in the mission.
- Present a preliminary discernment to the governing body of the church for their confirmation, correction, and support.

A case in point. Jan is a young mother of three children, about 30 years old. She invited her friend Ellen to attended Glendale Church with her. In conversation before the worship began, Ellen said, "I've sure felt lonely since we moved here from Chicago. Wish I could make a few more significant connections with other persons my age."

Jan responded sympathetically. During the next week, she had three additional conversations with members of the church who expressed the same need for friendship and a feeling of community. Sunday morning, the minister, Rev. Dr. Spottswood, spoke on the ways God gets our attention. When Jan heard him say, "God speaks by repetition through the things that happen in our lives," she wondered if God had spoken to her through a hunger for fellowship presented to her the past week.

Not too surprisingly, the idea that God was speaking to her did not go away. In fact, every day the next week the needs of these persons came into her mind. Drawing on her previous experience at the Elmwood Church in Omaha, she recalled how small groups gathering for prayer and Bible study not only deepened their faith, but also provided a ministry of fellowship.

Having a sense that God might be speaking to her in this convergence of ideas and expressed need and the memory of small groups, she decided to test it with Millie. She had met Millie soon after she became a member at Glendale and Millie's open spirit and obvious love for God impressed her.

After setting a meeting time with Millie, she began to organize her thoughts. When she reviewed Dr. Spottswood's sermon and her conversations with several lonely people, she came up with the persistent notion of forming a Bible study fellowship group. Then she wondered aloud what Millie thought about the idea. Jan experienced a mixture of delight and anxiety when Millie responded with unbridled enthusiasm. She even wanted to be part of the first group.

Jan's courage grew as she reflected on Millie's reaction, but before going to the pastor or the governing body of the church, she needed further confirmation. It occurred to her that the three couples with whom they met monthly for food and fellowship would also provide another forum to help her test God's guidance. When she shared her story with them, their response was similar to Millie's, though not quite as exuberant.

The next week she made an appointment with the minister. He listened patiently to her sense of call and promised to bring it to the attention of the governing body. After listening to the pastor's report of the different aspects of the call, the officials prayed and discussed Jan's discernment. They concurred with her that this seemed to be a call from God.

Jan received their confirmation with anxiety but they also offered her reassuring support and a promise to help. On the Sunday morning when the Bible study fellowship was announced, eight persons showed up for the first meeting. Inside her spirit Jan bubbled with joy at the mysterious ways of God.

No one illustration provides a perfect model for discernment of mission but perhaps this one will help your process along.

A Corroborative Witness

The Bible reports only two occasions in which Jesus cries. Once he cries in a cemetery while visiting the burial plot of a friend. Tears break forth again as he approaches the city of Jerusalem for the last time. If the essence of the Christian life is to become like Christ in every way — to identify with his passions, to be fueled by the causes that he uniquely champions, and to let our hearts be broken with the things that break his heart — then most of us are halfway home when it comes to tears. We need little prompting to cry in cemeteries. It doesn't feel nearly as natural, however, to shed tears while approaching major metropolitan areas.

I don't generally cry as I drive from the suburbs of Indianapolis toward the center of the city. Instead I turn away. I shake my head. I make sure I have enough gas before driving past the worst neighborhoods. The irony is that I grew up in a part of Indiana's capital now identified by police as the center of highest gang activity. When I drive down the streets of my childhood, I do so only in daylight. I sigh to myself, "I'm so glad to live miles away from these problems." Rarely is it my first response to cry . . . or to pray.

Jesus, however, was moved to tears as he came to the capital city of his homeland. "As he approached Jerusalem and saw the city, he wept over it" (Luke 19:41). Why? The next sentence says it all: "Jesus said, 'If you, even you, had only known this day what would bring you peace.'" Jesus brings peace. Jesus transforms human life. Yet at the gates of Jerusalem he knew those offers would be rejected. So he wept. Then he did the unimaginable. Jesus went into the city and died, providing the ultimate sacrifice to make peace a reality.

To call a local church into the mission of Jesus is to call its members into the same two behaviors. First we cry. Then we die. We let our hearts be broken with the things that break the heart of God. Then we die to the comfortable patterns of life that insulate us emotionally and geographically from those for whom Christ died.

It all begins with tears — not the occasional catch in the throat so easily synthesized by the well-crafted story — but from the explosion of emotion when we see the world, if only briefly, with divinely focused eyes. The church is called to weep for the sheer lostness of people. Something must whisper at us, or scream, that there are realities that cannot continue another day. Then God says, "Go! Trust me to provide the gifts and the time and the means to fulfill this vision for healing that's been laid upon your heart."

As a church leader, however, I feel as if I am always facing disheartening obstacles. In Zionsville we've found our passion to cry and to die for the mission of Christ thwarted by four factors. They happen to rhyme: *race, place, grace,* and *face.*

Race has drawn an invisible line across the north side of Indianapolis, three miles from the site of our church. In our community of seven thousand there are no more than ten families of color. Prompted by a burning desire to create interracial partnerships in ministry, a young businessman named Kent forged a relationship with the pastor of the Immanuel House of Prayer, an inner-city congregation in Indianapolis. Kent brought his family to worship at Immanuel, invited friends to come along as well, and patiently waited for me to catch his vision. Ultimately the two congregations began a relationship of swapping preachers and musicians, and the children of our churches — if only for a Sunday at a time — have now entered the new world of worshiping alongside each other as brothers and sisters of faith. Kent's broken heart and gentle persistence have blessed hundreds.

Place has traditionally separated baptized Christians from the masses who don't know the name of Jesus. For centuries, "those people" have been so far away that it's been hard to imagine personally encountering them in mission. They're not far away anymore. We say to our congregation, "You can go there. We can get you there." For little more than the cost of a round-trip airline ticket to Atlanta, a member of our church can wake up the next morning in Romania, where we have entered a partnership of evangelism, prayer, and support with a young, post-revolution congregation. In 1998 we endeavored to enlist 10 percent of our youth and adults — a tithe of our human resources — to invest at least seven days in mission ventures somewhere beyond the perimeter of our church property. When the challenge was presented on a Sunday morning, over 20 percent of the congregation signed on to serve in new places where the Spirit of God has preceded them.

Grace speaks to the Old World bias that our immeasurable blessings, both spiritual and material, are evidence that God's favor has been ordained to shine upon us while the rest of the globe goes wanting. Jesus counters with a statement of supreme challenge and terror: "To whom much is given, much is required." Reaching for the checkbook does not assuage responsibility. Christ longs for disciples who will join him on the crest of the hill overlooking Jerusalem, weeping for those who go to bed at night without peace. The public presentation of one child's stash of pennies — the rash act of one eight-year-old's huge heart to provide for others — did more to call our congregation into mission than any finely crafted Sunday message.

Face is the final barrier to joining Jesus in his global revolution. When I look at a sprawling city or a global demographics analysis sheet, I fail to see faces — faces to which I can relate. I see numbers and abstractions and problems I cannot fathom, and as a consequence I feel utterly inadequate to go serve six billion faceless people. I know, however, that God sees every face. God hears every cry. Our task challenges us to call the church to be God-like in its passion to bring love to people, even a face at a time.

On September 6, 1975, Thelma Perkins, a 38-year-old mother of three in Maryville, Tennessee, was assigned to the newborn intensive-care unit of the hospital where she had just become a nurse. That day a baby arrived with extraordinary needs. This little girl had light, curly brown hair, but a "face" that was nothing more than a shapeless mass of wet mucous membranes. She had no eyes, no nose, and only a ragged opening for breathing and feeding.

A few days later the ICU supervisor called a staff meeting and made one thing clear. "I don't want to hear any more talk about this baby's appearance," she said. "Her name is Alice. She has a purpose in this world, and we are going to treat her like every other newborn patient."

Thelma Perkins found herself drawn in love to this baby with no face. She talked and cooed to Alice, picked her up, cuddled her and loved her. Eventually she and her husband Ray became Alice's adoptive parents. They patiently taught her to sit and walk. Alice endured a series of operations through which surgeons fashioned her a face. In preschool she was taught to form words and at age seven could speak 250 of them. She learned how to play and live happily in her world.

The story of Ray and Thelma Perkins's unconditional love found its way into a *Reader's Digest* article in 1983. Fourteen years later one of the young moms in our church read it for the first time. Pam was so moved that she felt prompted to see if there was still a phone listing in Maryville, Tennessee, for a Ray Perkins. Even as she thought, "This is a crazy thing to do," Pam found herself dialing directory assistance. Moments later she was on the phone with Thelma Perkins, then age 59.

Thelma radiated a love for God. She related that Alice was due to graduate in a few months from the Tennessee School for the Blind, had a good sense of humor, and loved to go to church. Then she choked back tears, saying, "Alice was diagnosed a few years ago with a form of MS which was causing her to lose her hearing. Eventually she won't be able to walk." When asked about further prayer concerns, Thelma indicated the need to build an addition onto their home with a wheelchair entrance.

That night Pam shared the news of the phone call with her husband Bob. Without hesitation he said, "Let's offer to go help Ray build that addition." A few weeks later Bob and Pam and their family drove 350 miles to Maryville, Tennessee, and established construction plans with the Perkinses. News of the trip inspired the involvement of four other churches, two in Tennessee and two in Indiana. Suddenly dozens of people who were unknown to each other, separated by time and space, came together to do something incredible in Jesus' name — all for a girl who once literally had no face.

First we cry. Then we die, letting go of our old hang-ups of race, place, grace, and face. At last we come alive to the privilege of building a world in which everyone might know the peace that Jesus alone can provide.

QUESTIONS FOR REFLECTION AND DISCUSSION

1. How does your particular church seek to discern the will of God for its mission?
2. How does discernment contrast with using the tools of management for determining what the church will do?
3. How do the text of scripture, the context of the church, the gifts of people, and the revealing work of the Holy Spirit work in the process of discerning the mission of the church?
4. In your efforts to discern the will of God, how many of the criteria of discernment have you used? Recall specific instances when you have employed these criteria.
5. Pastor McDonald suggested that race, place, grace, and face provide critical aspects of discerning mission. How does each of these figure into your mission work?

CHAPTER SIX

Preaching to a Church
in the Spirit

PREACHING, REAL PREACHING, is Christ speaking through the voice of the preacher to those who worship God. Nothing compares to the experience of hearing Christ through a human voice. No preacher, once she has felt her lips utter the Word of Christ, can ever settle for her own recitation. A congregation that has listened to the Lord speak through a chosen servant will always feel cheated and hungry when the sermon lacks this transcendent Spirit. Even when the longing to hear Christ cannot be fully verbalized, the people of God know something has been lost or misplaced or neglected.

If we believe Christ inhabits the community that bears his name, and if we believe that he lives in members of his body, and if we believe he chooses, calls, and ordains some of these members to speak his Word to the congregation, then the call to be a preacher of the Word is an awesome calling. What task in all the world could be more challenging, and at the same time more humbling, than to speak for Christ? The church of the future will flourish as preachers of the Word embrace this astounding role and offer themselves to Christ that he may speak through them.

I have never written about preaching; I have elected to do so here because I believe preaching in the Spirit holds one of the essential keys for the creation and maintenance of a Church in the Spirit. I have chosen to write more directly to preachers about preaching to offer my suggestions and make a few observations. I consider myself neither a great preacher nor a learned homiletician, even though I have engaged in the task for over fifty years. In that half-century I have formed a few ideas and been grasped by several convictions I want to set forth.

In this brief essay I intend to offer a few insights about the person of the preacher — about who we are and how our being affects our preaching. I will reflect with you about receiving the Word of Christ, preparing the Word, and speaking the Word in a way that it echoes in the people.

The Preacher of the Word

You cannot be an effective preacher in a spiritually alive church without a conviction that you share in a task that belongs to another. The ministry belongs to Christ. You have been called to participate in his ministry. You did not choose to be a preacher, you were chosen. "You did not choose me, but I chose you, and ordained you" (John 15:16). No one can be a faithful preacher of the Word of Christ without this foundational conviction. As a preacher, you must be spiritually alive and growing in your awareness of the presence of Christ. Prayer, study, and reflection will aid you, but the Word of God must come to you from beyond yourself if you hope to address the conflicts, frustrations, and hungers of those who sit before you hopeful of hearing a whisper from God. I've listened to sermons, too painful to recall, when the word spoken floated on clouds beyond the grasp of the congregation. How tragic. How boring. How insulting to Christ.

These high-flying orators, who imagine the audience filled with their seminary professors and their ministerial heroes, deliver sermons to inform and impress them with their knowledge and clever delivery. But you, the true spokesperson for God, have been convicted that your own words matter very little because only God's Word communicates God. Yet, human words can indeed become the Word of God. Every preacher, from time to time, receives the confidence that God does in deed speak through him or her when someone remarks, "God spoke to me through your sermon this morning."

Christ in you makes possible your speaking for God, and he always longs to speak his Word through you. It is not as though we must persuade Christ, or compel him that he ought to speak through us. He wants to! Though he wills to speak through you to the congregation every worship day, nothing guarantees he will. Speaking for Christ requires preparation, but preparation does not guarantee that Christ will speak through you. Preaching requires prayer — hours of it. But praying does not guarantee that Christ will speak through your lips. In fact, nothing guarantees that Christ will speak his Word at a particular time or place because he always remains free to speak when and as he will. You are called to prepare your mind and heart to offer the Word you have received from Christ, but you must always trust Christ to speak to those persons present. You trust him to speak, but you cannot force him to speak. This powerlessness of every preacher both frustrates and liberates. The frustration arises out of our impotence to make the Word happen. But this hard reality also liberates us from the responsibility of what the preaching produces. Everything rests upon Christ.

So as you seek to become the voice of Christ, keep opening yourself to him. He will teach you about yourself; he will reveal himself to you. He will speak to you so that you may speak to the people. As you listen to Christ, he will say to the community what he wants them to hear. You can only offer this Word when you have been grasped by and filled with his Spirit, a precondition for the human word to become the Word of Christ.

The Preacher Receives the Word

How can you speak unless you have heard? You do not speak your own message, but the message of Christ; and you cannot speak it unless he has spoken it to you, and you have heard it. The truth of Christ comes to you. It seems to be a reality outside of you that appears spontaneously and challenges you. As Christ appears in this revelation of himself, you hear more than you realize at the moment. Have you not had moments when the reality of Christ came to you like that? Where was it? How did it come to you?

Did he speak to you through the text of scripture, in that flat text of words and punctuation marks? You pored over the text, listening for his Word to be spoken to the community. Did you hear him address you? Perhaps it is that tiny word in Jesus' sermon, "The light of the body is the eye." Suddenly you know that he is not talking about the natural eye, but the spiritual eye, about "seeing spiritually." Then, you recognize that spiritual sight, like natural sight, has been conditioned. You wonder how your way of seeing has been formed, especially the way you see God. Maybe this is a Word of Christ.

The Word of Christ heard in the text of scripture has also been conditioned and formed in the context of the church. The Word of God in scripture can also be heard in the members of the body of Christ. So, you listen for the Word in the text and also in the community. One is a textual word; the other a communal word. You hear the words spoken in the community through the needs, hungers, and hopes of the people. As you go about the parish, you wonder what Word God will speak to you through their dreams, hopes, needs, and hungers today.

Imagine you are visiting with a family where the woman has previously talked with you about being abused by her father. She welcomes your visit, and in the course of conversation she confesses her difficulty trusting God. After listening to her pain, you say, "Do you think there is a possible relationship between your father's physical abuse and your difficulty trusting God?" A light seems to click on in her mind.

You have prayer, say good-bye, and get in your car. As you drive away, it suddenly dawns on you that you also have heard the Word through this encounter. This woman's way of seeing disrupts her whole life. And the confession of difficulty trusting God connects with the text of scripture you read Monday morning, "The light of the body is the eye. . . ."

As you reflect more deeply on this text, you wonder how it relates to the kingdom of God. The text not only addresses individuals in the community of faith, but it also speaks of how the whole church sees God's providential concern in the unfolding of history and the large sweep of the Spirit in the kingdom of God. How does this text challenge the narrow, individualistic view of many members in the congregation? Does it challenge them to see God in a much larger arena?

After being grasped by this text and having your initial insight confirmed by your visit with this searching woman, you have begun to wonder how this text speaks to the larger needs in the congregation. Early in your preparation of the sermon, the potency of the text shifts to you, to your own way of seeing. Questions arise. How have my own experiences conditioned the way I hear this text? What diseases of the eye, my spiritual vision, do I have? You are not only a preacher of the gospel, after all; you are also a listener. Because you are a listener, this text begins to grow in your soul.

Although these illustrations may seem simplistic, I hope they add concreteness to my claim that the preacher of the Word must be a recipient of the Word. These four ways of receiving the Word unveil possible ways Christ speaks to the preacher. The Word of Christ may originate in the text, the context, or kingdom concerns, but in practice all four modalities eventually fuse together in the preacher and are proclaimed as the whole Word of God. Fusion comes as a gift, in a moment of revelation when the Spirit becomes flesh in the preacher. When this incarnation occurs, the Word of Christ is conceived in your heart and life, and it can no longer be spoken as some truth outside of you, only as testimony.

Have you not experienced this reception of the Word in an incarnation of sorts — an encounter with Christ in which the Word was received, gestated, and birthed? In this incarnational event you become one with the text, you are joined to the message. When you speak this incarnate Word, the congregation recognizes and affirms its authenticity. This receptivity to the text gives preaching power and integrity.

The way incarnation occurs is as unpredictable as the angel's visit to Mary. It often comes when you least expect it. You may be looking for inspiration for a sermon, or visiting a member, or reading about a crisis in society, or idly watching television. The Word comes to you in its own way and time.

The Word gets your attention, comes into consciousness with a greater strength than other stimuli around you. The Word evokes interest, makes a connection with you in some manner, and draws you to itself until you embrace the idea. This utterance of a Word of God conveys energy that excites and fires your imagination. You hear yourself asking, "How does this word speak to me? How does it speak to members of the congregation? What are the needs in our context that it addresses? What kingdom vision does it call forth?" This process of musing over the Word nurtures the truth with which you have been impregnated. As the Word grows, it kicks, turns, and develops until delivery.

The Preacher Imagines the Word

To deliver this incarnate Word, you had best imagine the Word as narrative. Delivering the Word as narrative does not suggest telling a series of stories. The Word itself is storied, having a beginning followed by movement and an ending. The sermon, as narrative, contrasts sharply with a lecture. The sermon engages the congregation, leads them through the truth conceived, provides moments for thought and reflection, and invites a response. At its best, the sermon invites the listener into an awareness of God and leaves him or her standing before the holy with a sense of the mystery.

The lecture paradigm provides data, making logical, persuasive points aimed at convincing the hearer of the urgency of the truth proclaimed. Perhaps this old style has its place; but narrative has the advantage of speaking to the whole person, and it invites many surprises. Narrative also creates images so that the sermon penetrates the hearer's personal depths through intuition and imagination. The opening words of the sermon invite the hearer into the narrative and they seek to connect the narrative life of the listener to the narration of the Word spoken.

The narrative Word unfolds in a manner that invites the listener and the preacher into truth. Like a drama, the narrative sermon has movement, appropriate transitions, and a sense of expectancy. So as the story line of the narrative unfolds, the preacher gives the listeners space to wonder, to muse over the images, and to make connections between the spoken words and their own lives. As a sensitive preacher you will invite your listeners to follow the narrative to deeply personal dimensions. A good narrative, creatively imagined, will provide serendipity.

Some aspects of imagining the story line of the sermon include: reading, researching, exegeting the text, and brooding over the text in the context while considering its inherent movement. The task of preparing the sermon for delivery forces you to order the dramatic unfolding of ideas so that they present the truth in an interesting, compelling, focused, and incisive manner. Your task may be aided by a few questions like: What is the one thing I hope this sermon will convey to the listener? (Making one point and having it heard and appropriated would be a powerfully effective sermon!) How will I begin? What are the three or four major movements in the sermon? How will I make smooth transitions from one movement to the next? What images will help my hearer see the ideas I am presenting (i.e., what metaphors and similes)? How will I hold interest, create anticipation, provide a rest stop, change the mood or movement? What will I leave in their minds when I finish? What do I hope they will do as a result of this Word?

Recall the experiences of receiving the Word. I will use that material to illustrate the process of imagining the Word as narrative.

The first movement. Engage the people where they are in "seeing." "Have you ever considered how important your eyes are?" Explore briefly what it would mean to live without vision. This is like the first scene in your drama — a need established.

Second movement. Connect the need for our vision with what Jesus says about the eye being the lamp of the body, the meaning of light and darkness, the healthy and unhealthy eye. Suggest the truth of these statements at a natural level, but underscore how these ideas are pleading another message. Explore the metaphorical dimensions of the light, the diseased eye, and healthy eye.

Third movement. Recall your visit to one of the parishioners, your own encounter with the text, and your awareness of a limited vision in the congregation. Let these situations ground your text in felt needs. Begin to draw your listeners into the awareness of their need for seeing more clearly.

I can think of three ways you may draw the listeners into the text. Ask them direct questions about their vision. Are they near-sighted, far-sighted, astigmatic, do they have double vision, etc.? Help them identify their own need. Or, you could wonder with them about how they see. A short vignette of a person who had been blind for a time and received her sight would provide a metaphor for them. The experience could be a metaphor for spiritual insight also.

Finally, the last movement extends an invitation for your hearers to respond to the message. One conclusion might be to invite the congregation to bring their distorted vision to Jesus, like the blind man he touched who saw persons as trees walking. Narrate the coming of Jesus as if each of them is this person, this man — as if Jesus touches them here today.

Do you see how this text can become storied? You open with an exploration of poor vision, a loss of vision that leads into Jesus' exploration of the woeful consequences of visual impairment, both naturally and spiritually. You conclude by showing how Jesus heals the visually impaired and send them on their way with hope.

Working with the text in this way describes what I mean by imagining the text as narrative. You imagine the vision of the people to whom you preach, lead them into Jesus' truth about vision, invite them to own their need or confess that they may need to see more clearly, and you conclude by helping them walk in the steps of a blind man to the Lord Jesus who gives us sight.

Write the sermon. Write it clearly, sequentially, cogently, simply, and logically (to you). Rewrite it until it flows like a stream. When you finish editing the sermon, mull it over, write notes on the pages, dirty up the manuscript. A clean manuscript lacks work! Then take this storied text into the pulpit and tell it to the people with enthusiasm.

The Preacher Immerses the Word in Prayer

You long for the sermon to be a Word from God, for God to speak to the people. You want to have God speak through you. In the presence of God, remember that this is not your word, but God's. It is as though

Christ has laryngitis and has asked you to speak in his place. The closer you are to the Spirit, the more your consciousness fuses with the Word, the more accessible you are to the Spirit of God. Your relation to God does not guarantee that God will speak the Word through you, but when you prepare your mind, open your heart, become receptive to the Spirit, surely God will fill you and speak through your words. The preparation of the soul is as crucial as the preparation of your mind.

To prepare your heart, enter into your spiritual center, the place of meeting with God. Bring the Word that has been given you into the divine presence. You take the message to God for God's blessing. Spread out the Word before God. With a sermon lying on the table before the Lord for a final edit, listen imaginatively to the Spirit. Pay careful attention to the words, images, and directions that come to your awareness.

In the presence of the one who speaks, rehearse the sermon, tell the story to God. Visualize the drama unfolding. Become aware that God sees you, sees the sermon, and feels the intensity of your desire to speak this Word of God to the people.

I find it helpful to brood over each point until I feel connected to its truth. I then move to the next and the next until I have prayed the whole sermon. Again, I review the major points with my eyes closed, yet I can see the sermon unfolding and I feel it taking hold of my life. A mysterious fusion between God, the Word, and my consciousness often occurs.

In this holy place, I wait for the Spirit to breathe upon the sermon, to give it a life of its own. Just as one blows into the mouth of a drowned person to give him life, I pray for the Spirit to breathe into the flat narrative until it is alive in my memory and dancing in my imagination.

Do not expect the same experience each time you pray the sermon. The breath of God comes with great variety, but your part is to commit the Word to God and ask the Spirit to speak to the people as you proclaim God's Word.

The Preacher Delivers the Word

Despite all you do to hear the Word and appropriate the Word in your life, the time comes when you stand before the people and speak in the place of Christ. When you stand to speak, trust the presence of Christ to speak through you to the people of God. Think of yourself as a conduit mediating the Word of God to the congregation, knowing the power is not yours but God's. God, and God alone, makes the choice to speak or not speak through your human words. Do not pay too much attention to your spirit as you preach. Focus on the people. You are not preaching a sermon. You are speaking to people for Christ.

Think about the storyteller as a model for preaching. The storyteller knows the narrative by heart and would never think of reading the story to an audience. Because the storyteller knows the narrative so well, she does not need to tell it word for word, she can improvise in response to her audience. The storyteller, no matter how many times she has told the story, never sounds canned or dull. The one telling a story speaks with the listeners and has a keen sense of timing and emphasis. She constantly engages her audience, evoking questions, inviting wonder, and enchanting them with the tale so that the experience never grows dull. The story moves with a rhythm appropriate for the listeners. Sermon telling would provide a welcome relief to many weary congregations.

As you preach the Word, forget yourself and let the narrative take control. Having a sense of the Spirit speaking through you does not matter. You are engaged with the truth, telling the story, uttering words that have taken hold of you and now have become incarnate in your life.

Never forget your audience. You are telling this God-inspired story to searching people sitting expectantly before you. You are not rehearsing a narrative from memory but participating in a living drama — you are speaking for God, for Christ in the Spirit. Getting this storied sermon into the consciousness of your listeners will transform them. As you speak, pay attention to the mood of your audience; notice their receptivity and response. Talk with the people. Pray that everyone before you feels as if you are speaking only to him or her.

At times you will feel an anointing of the Spirit, which sharpens your consciousness and gives you an authority and boldness not your own. Preaching in the Spirit inspires a joyous freedom that liberates your imagination and fills both you and the congregation with energy. On one occasion the Word will have a sharpness that cuts into the mind and heart of the congregation. On another, it will be like a magnet that draws persons into its transformative sphere. Imaginative preaching has the character of an ecstatic dance with God.

When the Spirit of Prophecy takes hold of you, do not be distracted by the powerful presence of God working through you. Keep with the story, stay focused on the message and the people; permit God to speak, as God will. Giving too much attention to the working of the Spirit will detract from the Word that God speaks to the people.

The Preacher Listens for the Word's Echo

The freedom you experience preaching the Word comes from the sturdy conviction that the Word belongs to God and not to you. Both the Word and its results are God's. Do not judge the sermon by the accuracy of your listeners' correct hearing. God sometimes speaks a Word you never considered. Preaching and hearing will always be a mystery to you; people will thank you for words you did not know you spoke, and probably didn't.

When the sermon has been delivered, attend what the people say. Dismiss the casual chat about how good or how interesting the sermon may have been. Attend the persons who give evidence that the Word took lodging in their minds or hearts. Look into the eyes of the people; pay attention to the emotion with which they speak. Note those you should call or visit.

Reflect on the responses you receive. What do the responses say to you about the message you thought you were giving? Did the congregation confirm your word? Did they hear the word you intended? Were there echoes of the Word in conversations during the week?

Doubtless you have noticed me struggling to describe the experience of the Holy Spirit grasping the consciousness of the preacher and raising it to a new level. In that ecstatic encounter with the holy presence, a transformation takes place. We have been grasped by the Divine Mystery, and we are left with a sense of awe.

A Corroborative Witness

Once, while staying in Orlando, Florida, Mary Sue and I got what a couple of Hoosiers would call the chance of a lifetime. The local news affiliates announced that the launch of the space shuttle *Columbia* was a "go" for 3:18 P.M. on what was predicted to be a beautiful afternoon. In fact, the reporter threw in that this was only the second time in the history of the shuttle program that the "launch window" had a 100 percent possibility of perfect weather. That's when we made our decision: we would hop into our rental car and drive the fifty-five miles from Orlando to the Kennedy Space Center to see this spectacle for ourselves.

We budgeted plenty of time to make the trip. After a leisurely lunch we got onto the Florida Bee Line and headed east — and immediately merged into a logjam of hundreds and hundreds of cars. At first I figured we were stuck in a tollbooth back-up, but the congestion extended beyond the booth all the way to the horizon. Within thirty minutes it dawned on us that we had voluntarily become part of a fifty-five-mile-long traffic jam, and were surrounded by thousands of people who wanted to see precisely what we had come to see.

We crept across the state, starting and stopping, until at 3:15 P.M. we were still at least twenty miles from our goal. That's when the myriad of rental cars and minivans around us began to park along the roadside. We did the same. People turned up their radios, got out their cameras, gathered in clusters on the shoulder, and looked vaguely toward the east, across the Florida swampland. We could hear the countdown: ". . . three, two, one . . . ," and I wondered what exactly we'd be able to see so far away.

It was incredible. A bright orange flame on top of a pillar of smoke rose from the ground at a speed much faster than I thought possible. It all lasted no more than a half minute; the shuttle disappeared from our view into the haze. During that time, however, the gawking group of strangers with whom we were standing were overwhelmed by a staggering silence, punctuated only by an occasional, "Wow!" Just as quickly, reality returned. As if on cue we all jumped back into our cars, cutting across medians and racing to get an advantage over everybody else in the traffic jam that was now headed west. But for just a few moments we had had a mutual encounter: together we had experienced awe.

Why did so many people think a thirty-second thrill was worth the hassle? In the middle of the state that advertises more entertainment highs than any other, people were famished for the opportunity to stand, even at a distance, in the presence of something awesomely larger and more powerful than themselves.

That, I believe, is essentially why people come to hear sermons. Presented with an ever-growing menu of self-fulfillment opportunities on Sunday mornings, men and women willingly endure the hassles and distractions of coming alongside other worshipers to hear, just possibly — if only for a few moments — the voice of One whose presence overshadows and infuses the rest of life's race with meaning. They come for an experience of awe.

In a world of techno-sophistication that daily erodes the last vestiges of wonder in ordinary life, hungry souls yearn for a message from God. The mandate of the preacher is to live with such integrity in the presence of God and to study the Word with such energy and giftedness that when he or she finally stands to speak, those who listen will experience an in-breaking of the invisible world that literally brings their frantic lives to a stop, and sends them away transformed by their response to the gospel.

For me, preaching has always been a messy business. I fully agree with the sentiment, "Unless God speaks today, I have nothing to say." So far, however, that hasn't prevented me from opening my mouth in countless worship services with little or no idea what the Holy Spirit might be up to. I am grimly aware of the darker side of my homiletic life — the cesspool of ego needs, the consuming desire for affirming handshakes and complimentary "well done's" at the door. All too often I head for home wondering, *How did I come across today? What did they think of that turn of phrase? Will they mention my name at Sunday brunch?*

I know that on Sunday mornings either I get out alive or the truth gets out alive. There can be only one survivor. Either I preach in such a way that I neurotically reach for the assurance that I am still loved and needed, or I prayerfully prepare and stand in such a way that God's truth has a genuine chance to be heard through my voice. Worshipers hunger to hear God's voice. God's voice is heard, albeit "stuttering," through our voices.

Along the way I've consciously surrendered several illusions I cherished about preaching. The first is that my role was to reduce the teaching of Jesus to principles, and then present them in outline form with suitable illustrations. Amazingly, I had to read the Gospels many times before I noticed the obvious: that a huge percentage of our Lord's teaching is in story form. Both Old and New Testaments are built on the foundation of great stories of God's work — the delivery of God's people from slavery in Egypt and the delivery of God's people from sin-slavery through the cross — stories that are memorialized in rituals (Passover and communion) designed for continual retelling and re-experiencing. Why do listeners inevitably look up and reconnect when the preacher begins a story? Because God has wired our minds and hearts to hear the Voice in the context of stories. Consequently I have worked harder in sermons at demonstrating specific links between the stories of individuals, our church's story, and the ongoing account of God's work among us.

A second illusion that died hard was the notion that somehow a twenty to twenty-five minute exposition, once a week, would effectively transform a human life that is being molded and conditioned by seven hours of television daily, and is bombarded relentlessly by spectacular visual advertisements designed by some of the brightest minds in our culture. American teenagers, whose attention spans have been measured at between six to eight minutes, aren't likely to make it through point one of my finely crafted sermon if there aren't visual or story-related oases strategically placed along the way.

"Great books" no longer provide the common culture that once could be assumed among churchgoers. Today in America the common culture is provided by movies, TV shows, and commercials. I am amazed at the instant recognition and camaraderie that unites a group of adults as they watch a two-minute clip from "Sister Act" or "Forrest Gump." If I'm not willing to utilize the technology that provides such images for the sake of speaking with greater impact and relevance about the truth, I can be sure that someone else will be utilizing it to sell my flock cereal or deodorant.

Effective preaching in the twenty-first century will require full appreciation for the multisensory, mosaic ways in which people are increasingly making sense of their worlds. Protestants have classically relied on the spoken word alone, placed on the lips of a seminary-trained cleric, offered in a linear and rational style to a group of people whose role it is to understand, appreciate, and assimilate the message. Anyone who attends worship services that regularly feature a "time with the children" is aware of the fact that it's infinitely easier to remember the simple *visual* object lesson that is presented to our youngest learners than it is to retain even the basic outline of the "grown-up" message. If I cannot personally remember the details of what I preached just three weeks earlier, why should I fantasize that my listeners still remember?

In our efforts to do a better job of communicating on Sunday mornings — to provide multiple points at which those present might better hear the voice of God — we have agreed that every worship hour should revolve around a stated theme. Every element of the service — sermon, songs, prayers, drama, call to worship, time with the children — spotlights the theme. The front margin of the bulletin states, for example, *As we continue our look at the "irregular emotions" that characterize our lives, our focus this morning is on the fear that makes us want to hide ourselves from God and from each other.* From such a theme springs a multitude of worship expressions and experiences, utilizing as much creativity and as many senses as possible, to reach the minds and hearts of the worshipers with the truth that God's perfect love abolishes human fear. As a preacher I can draw from the music, dramas, cinematic clips, or prayer requests of the morning to help demonstrate the truthfulness of that theme.

Finally, I must demonstrate why there are lines to cross and decisions to make, and why those decisions have relevance to what might happen next Thursday. Otherwise our worship services become just another experience to throw into the hopper, unfiltered or indistinguishable from the multitude of other personal experiences available in our culture.

A man in his thirties once introduced himself after visiting one of our services. He asked, "Do you meet with people during the week?" "I do," I answered. Looking around, he asked, "Do you have an office where you have those meetings?" "Right down that hall," I answered, beginning to grasp that this was perhaps the first church encounter this man had ever had. When we met a few days later he said, "I'll only take a few moments of your time. Recently we learned that my daughter has a serious illness. Fortunately it was detected and diagnosed in time, and she's going be okay. I've truly been filled with gratitude about this, and I feel the need to say Thank-You. Here's what I'd like to ask: Who am I supposed to thank for this wonderful thing that has happened in my family?" The rest of our time together we talked about the God of mercy and grace who alone is worthy of our deepest gratitude.

Who are we supposed to thank? The ultimate measure of our worship and preaching is not whether it generates an experience, but whether it helps make the invisible become visible, and connects the real-life stories of those who participate with the reality of the Triune God.

QUESTIONS FOR REFLECTION AND DISCUSSION

(Gather a trusted group of friends and leaders to discuss these questions with the pastor. Both pastor and lay persons should answer the questions.)

1. What are we expecting during the worship hour?
2. How does our minister seek to speak for God?
3. When do we most often experience the presence of God in the preaching?
4. How is Pastor McDonald's experience in preaching similar to preaching in your church?

CHAPTER SEVEN

An Inclusive Church
in the Spirit

H OW TO BECOME an inclusive, multicultural congregation may
be one of the strongest challenges facing mainline churches. A
survey of the mainline congregations reveals that most of them are
quite homogeneous; they are class churches or ethnic churches or suburban churches. As a result of their monolithic makeup they have lost
the richness of diversity, the openness to change, certain possibilities of
growth, and the complete fulfillment of Christ's mission to the world.
The search for inclusivity challenges the status quo of the mainline
churches and their unconscious exclusivity, both of which lead to
death.

The Mission of Jesus Christ

Without a doubt Jesus Christ's mission focused on the whole world,
not a select nation or group. All four Gospels and the Acts of the Apostles present the clear vision of a church intended to be universal and
inclusive in scope. Review the missionary practices of Jesus himself: he
came to bring life to the world, the whole world including Jews and
Gentiles; he ministered to persons regardless of their social standing;

he attended to women and children. A closer look at the ministry of Jesus reveals he gave priority to the broken, excluded, and marginalized persons who came into his sphere.

The Book of Acts records Peter's first sermon, which addressed persons from seventeen nations. But the inclusiveness of the gospel does not stop there. Very early the faith of Christ broke out of the Jewish strictures. The expansion began with Cornelius the centurion, who was a god-fearer but still an uncircumcised believer. His obedience to the command to send messengers to beckon Simon Peter resulted in the Gentiles hearing the gospel. A few years into his ministry Paul, after being rejected and persecuted by Jews, turned his full attention to the Gentiles. As a consequence he became the apostle to the Gentiles and established churches in scores of non-Jewish settings. The actions of both Peter and Paul pushed the church out of its Jewishness and made it a church for all peoples. In nearly every letter Paul argues for an inclusive church.

Paul believed the death of Jesus created a new society composed of many disparate groups — Jews and Gentiles, bond and free, women and men, wealthy and poor. This new society was called into being by the proclamation of the gospel; it was neither Jew nor Gentile but a "new creation" composed of all persons. Paul called this new creation the body of Christ. The Jesus who lived and ministered in the flesh was now risen and present in the Spirit to incarnate himself in a new body, a communal body, an inclusive body — his body on earth. The inclusion of all classes and types of persons in this body caused it to stand in sharp contrast to the society that based relations upon honor and shame.

For example, in the society of Paul's day a wealthy man used his prestige and honor to shame the poor and powerless. When he, for instance, gave a party, the seating was arranged so that the rich and respectable sat at the head table. In a descending order persons were seated from the head table out to the periphery of the dinner party. The closer they sat to the host, the greater honor they had been granted. The uninvited were left outside to look in upon the gala occasion. This elitist attitude gives explosive power to the stories of Jesus — stories about being invited from the margin of the group to the head table, about the man who sent servants into the highways and hedges to invite the blind, the sick, and the lame. Of course, all these persons were excluded from social acceptance in Jesus' world.

The "body of Christ" metaphor gathers up quite well the concerns Paul had for a new society united in Jesus. Even if the world does not hear the gospel and turn to Christ, the church will be a spearhead of the kingdom, a model of God's intention for society. In the church the marginalized and broken pieces of humanity have been reconciled with God and welcomed into Christ's community. These estranged persons have been included, not on their own merits, but by the grace of God. On those occasions *when the church is truly the church,* it is a haunting reminder of the possibility of all persons living together in love and harmony. This vision of a new society that claims a place for all kinds of persons is, perhaps, as revolutionary as God's forgiveness of the foulest of sinners. In its life the church demonstrated this new social arrangement as a foretaste of the kingdom of God.

Note how clearly Paul states the inclusive character of the body of Christ. In the letter to the Galatians he wrote, "For in Christ Jesus you are all children of God through faith. As many of you as were baptized into Christ have clothed yourselves with Christ. There is no longer Jew or Greek, there is no longer slave or free, there is no longer male and female; for all of you are one in Christ Jesus. And if you belong to Christ, then you are Abraham's offspring, heirs according to the promise" (Gal. 3:26-29). What a profound and daring affirmation to these believers! And what a challenging truth for us in our culture-bound congregations!

The inclusive church that Paul describes cannot come into being without a transcendent referent, that is, a theological vision that stands outside and beyond all earthly values and powers. This new center of existence must be such a powerful bearer of the holy that it shocks human reason and subverts all social norms. This referent must also blast pride at its roots and bring humankind to a state of humility that enables each to see value in the other. Nothing less can call forth a new humanity, erase boundaries, and unite persons in a new society. I believe the love of God revealed in Jesus as the one who loves the world enough to die for it, is that kind of transcendent referent. The early church acknowledged this powerful referent in the sacraments of baptism and Eucharist.

In the Church Catholic and in the mainline congregations, this transcendent referent has been baptism, the sacramental rite that dissolves status and unites persons to Christ and to each other. In most congregations the depth of meaning has been drained from this unifying sacrament. Consider it. To receive the water of baptism means persons have died to self and to their own life; it means they are buried with Christ in his death. But, it also implies resurrection from the tomb *with* Christ. This resurrection into a new life means living our life in a Christ-like way: a new person, a new creation, a new way of life! Baptism means beginning life all over again!

In mainline congregations baptism has been trivialized by making the sacrament an empty ritual or by failing to nurture the meaning of baptism in children and youth. Reclaiming the true meaning of baptism just might abolish the easy invasion of the Christian community by a secular culture. The lack of knowledge of both the faith and spiritual formation leads to the expansion of a powerless, cultural congregation. In this manner the transcendent referent has been obscured.

Evangelical churches have made the conversion experience, not baptism, this transcendent referent. To be born anew is an experience of dying to self and rising in Christ; it requires us to put off the old self and to put on the new. Thus, conversion provides evangelical Christians a common experience and a shared language to describe their experience of Christ. Conversion also serves as the uniting power for the converted. Because of the homogeneous nature of most evangelical congregations, however, conversion fails to transform these bodies into diverse and inclusive congregations.

In Pentecostal churches this transcendent referent has been the baptism in the Spirit, an experience of the holy that creates a bond, provides a common understanding, and offers a power that enables persons in the Spirit to cast off old identities and become one in the Spirit of Christ. In my judgment the Pentecostals have been more successful at the task of inclusivity than either the Catholics, mainline congregations, or evangelicals. In the mainline one wonders if the baptismal symbol has not died, thus losing its power to communicate or mediate the transcendent. And in the evangelical churches the experience of conversion has often become culturally domesticated, voiding the power to transform the vision of the converted. In recent years the Roman Catholic Church has taken decisive measures to reclaim the significance of this rite of initiation. Perhaps there is hope.

The sacrament of the Lord's Supper, Eucharist, or Holy Communion also contains this openness to the holy and can serve as the medium for creating the new community and its unity in the Spirit. Unfortunately, the Eucharist has suffered a similar fate to baptism.

The Lord's Supper in mainline churches often becomes a memorial in which Christ's death is recalled; in the Catholic Church it becomes a mere ritual, experienced without the power of faith. Evangelical churches neglect the Eucharist in favor of the Word; Pentecostals discount ritual and embrace experience. Through abuse, misunderstanding, and neglect, the church loses two powerful rituals that, if properly understood and shared, have the power to transform persons and create unity. The recovery of the deeper meaning of baptism and Eucharist may be a pathway to an inclusive Church in the Spirit.

Inclusivity and Survival

For the mainline congregations, inclusivity is not only a matter of faithfulness to Christ and the mission of the church (which is the proper motivation), but a matter of sheer survival.

Mainline congregations have long been captive to the homogeneous unit principle, that is, the aim to create congregations of like-minded persons. Since the church growth movement has adopted this principle as one of its core values, it has simultaneously announced a practical principle and revealed to mainline congregations what they have long practiced unconsciously. Without self-consciously articulating this principle, or intentionally adopting it as the norm for building churches, mainline congregations have nevertheless practiced it without a flaw. Examine almost any mainline congregation. Everyone looks alike, dresses alike, drives a prestige automobile, eats at the same popular restaurants, and values the same goals and experiences. A casual glance reveals the lack of social diversity.

Not only have these mainline churches blindly followed the "people like us" principle, but quite unconsciously they have become captive to an elitism that excludes those who are not like us. So persons from different social strata who embrace other values and who represent an alien culture and experience cannot find a place in the churches of most mainline denominations. Even when these congregations claim to welcome everyone, it becomes obvious to the outsiders that they simply do not fit. Honestly, does not this poor witness and lack of receptivity to diversity reveal the cultural foundation of our churches? I believe this to be reason enough for us to recover a conviction of the living Christ who died for all as the foundation of the church's life. And it strongly argues for the recovery of baptism and Eucharist as the mediators of his presence and power.

Most congregations in the mainline have focused on one or two social strata from which members are drawn. While on occasion we may spill over into the social grouping closest to us, we are nervous about the presence of these strangers and they soon drop out. We dare not venture too far into the next strata lest we create an imbalance in the church's culture.

I recall spending a weekend in an old First Church, located at the edge of an Army base. The new minister had worked hard to include enlisted men and women in the life of the congregation. Most of them did not look like the members of First Church. Their children were not well-behaved, and their need for the church was very different from the persons who had been in the church all their lives. These "different" people created anxiety within the membership. The jury is still out regarding the ability of this old church to open itself to them and welcome them into its fellowship.

The church's bondage to the homogeneous unity principle suggests that it is grounded in, and informed and molded by, the dominant culture more than by Christ. So we make decisions, admit members, and develop programs according to their social acceptability rather than by following the leadership of Jesus Christ. What is needed today? Do we not need to return to Christ our foundation, embrace his Spirit, and proceed toward a new day under leadership?

A source of much unrest comes perhaps from the dissolution of the culture without, and our loss of cohesiveness within the church; cultural confusion spills over into the church and disrupts its ministry. Since we have sacralized the cultural norms, confusion results when they begin to change. If we do not disengage from cultural norms and connect with Jesus Christ who is the source, life, and unity of the church, we may, and perhaps should, face extinction.

The context demands a culturally inclusive church. Again this is a survival issue. My denomination, the Presbyterian Church (USA), and other mainline churches can no longer think of themselves as class churches made up of wealthy, educated people who control the economic, social, and political power structures. If we are to survive as mainline churches, we must open ourselves to diversity and become a truly inclusive Church in the Spirit of Christ. The kinds of persons who have composed mainline congregations have usually been white, middle-, and upper-middle-class individuals situated in white-collar jobs. The number of persons matching this description is shrinking. If mainline congregations expect to survive the twenty-first century, they must come to grips with the demographic changes in the century ahead.

Today nearly half the persons entering seminary are female. In the next century, half or more of the ministers will likely be women. Women coming into ministry today are confronted with a male-dominated church, the use of male language, male leadership, and male control. The presence of women in our collegium calls us to be inclusive not only of those different folks outside the church but those female folk on the inside. For the sake of harmony, for the sake of unity, for the sake of effectiveness, and for the sake of faithfulness, mainline congregations must find ways to soften male domination and open leadership roles to all members and pastors.

Inclusivity insists that we also look at the generations that have sprung from our own members who are still, for the most part, outside the church. Most of them lack any experience in the church, knowledge of the faith, or even the language of the faith. Most are self-centered in their interests; they distrust institutions, and they have no history of, nor inclination toward, benevolence. If we are to be faithful as a church, we must understand these children of our lost members, and how to connect with them in an effective, transformative way. Because they form the largest segment of the unchurched, these are the persons we are compelled to reach in the new century.

The missionary imperative also demands an inclusive congregation. The twentieth century has witnessed the demise of colonialism and paternalistic mission to the developing world. Paternalism has given way to partnership. Partnership also has radical implications for doing church at home.

When we partner with churches overseas, they expect of us the same integrity we have demanded of them. Take the color of most mainline congregations, for example. If an African visits our congregation and does not shut his eyes, he will wonder where his people are in our church. It is not a matter of black shortages. Or, if our African brother visits us, he will look at the affluent lifestyle of our members and wonder how this witnesses to the gospel of compassion when so many in his country are starving. Or, he will engage a few members in conversation about the faith, and when they are reluctant to talk about the faith, he will wonder why they were not prepared for their baptism and confirmation. When we seek to do mission in North America, what can save us from paternalism in our service to the poor unless we have persons like those we seek to serve who are willing to link up with us and serve those who are unlike us?

A Corroborative Witness

Every church faces the very visible challenges of becoming more inclusive along the lines of race and economic standing. It's equally valid that we stretch out hands of grace to those who are essentially *invisible* in our midst, who feel pushed out of the center of what we say we are endeavoring for God. Our indifference to their presence — worse still, our blindness to their walking away — is an indictment of our claim to be God's children. Why? Because Jesus recognized, made time for, intentionally sought the companionship of, ate dinner with, and lavished his love upon those on life's periphery. His "wasting" of valuable ministry time on the "sick" became a religious scandal of the first order — a behavior that our churches scandalously fail to imitate to this day.

Several years ago I got a laugh when I looked at the religion section of our local paper. One of the church ads presented a little italicized motto at the bottom. Its author had intended to say, "An open and affirming church." Instead the line read, "An open and *infirming* church." How sad and how true. All too often we've made the sick feel sicker and the odd person out feel odder still.

The list of those who feel excluded includes the nineteen-year-old who didn't go to college like the rest of his friends; the family embarrassed about their low-rent apartment; the introverted woman who doesn't glow angelically like "all the other women" at the midweek Bible study; the divorced; the underemployed; the spiritually unconvinced; the dyslexic man who avoids small groups for fear he'll be asked to read aloud.

Painfully and slowly it began to dawn on me that our church, in the midst of celebrating the arrival of so many of "our kind" of people, had unwittingly come to rely on evangelistic nets with selective mesh. By not *intentionally* reaching for those beyond our circle of comfort we had co-opted Jesus' sorting role at the end of the age. We were doing the sorting just fine on our own, thank you.

The grief that such behavior must cause our Lord hit home recently when Mary Sue and I, returning from a church retreat, stopped at a fast food restaurant to grab lunch. We chose a national chain we hadn't patronized for years. The food was great and it occurred to us we could easily become regular customers again. Later that same day, however, Mary Sue's stomach began to send out interesting and dramatic distress signals. After wrestling with the dark side of biology for about four hours, we weren't nearly as eager to go back to that restaurant as we were before. That's the danger inherent in franchising. That restaurant chain may have great national advertising, product development, and market strategy, but everything falls apart if one worker in one outlet in Indiana thinks it's okay to leave the mayonnaise out all night. It's enough to give the CEO an upset stomach.

Jesus has franchised his message and his ministry to the local church, but so often our efforts publicly undermine his credibility. Given the opportunity to make a first impression on his behalf, we stumble. How might congregations narrow the gap between the Name we carry and the less-than-gracious ways we treat people?

At Zionsville we've pursued several strategies. First, we're committed to a constant public emphasis on what brings all of us before God on a level playing field: the fact that we are *rescued by grace,* not by cleverness, checking accounts, privilege, or pedigree. When we look in the mirror or when we look right or left on a Sunday morning, what we're seeing are persons extravagantly loved by God and who therefore have infinite value. Inclusiveness doesn't spring from duty or pity, but from a theology of grace fearlessly accepted and ruthlessly applied. Regularly during the announcements that precede worship we declare, "Our one message is that the unconditional love of God is extended to you right now through Jesus Christ . . . and we hope that during this service that message comes through loud and clear."

Second, we take time to *interview guests* and prospective members. Did they feel welcomed when they arrived? Could they find their way around? Did the services and sermons make sense? How long did it take before this church felt like home? Newcomers, who by definition stand on the outside at the moment of their arrival, are the resident experts on what it's really like to try to find a place in the fellowship of our church.

Third, we place a strong and recurrent emphasis on *spiritual gifts,* citing the truth that any believer who walks through our door is bringing a blend of abilities, passions, and experiences that *no one in the kingdom* has ever seen or evidenced before. What a glorious equalizer! The New Testament metaphor of the body is proof that any notion of an exclusive "inside circle" or "core" in a church is pure fantasy. In *The Message* Eugene Peterson brilliantly renders 1 Corinthians 12:17-18: "I also want you to think about how this keeps your significance from getting blown up into self-importance. For no matter how significant you are, it is only because of what you are a *part* of. An enormous eye or a gigantic hand wouldn't be a body, but a monster. What we have is one body with many parts, each its proper size and in its proper place."

Fourth, we *intentionally create opportunities* to be more inclusive of those with special needs and sensitivities. Every seventh couple struggles to fulfill the dream of bearing children. In a church that is filled with young families, virtually every week brings another child baptism or dedication. Faces may sag or turn away as I call attention to the single rose on the communion table announcing another birth. For those in the throes of infertility, worship can feel like a cruel reminder of failure or even imply divine rejection. From time to time our corporate prayer focuses directly on the needs of would-be parents — especially on Mother's Day and Father's Day — and we invite the congregation to help carry the unique pain of this reality that leaves some couples feeling excluded.

Some years ago I received a letter from a newer member of our church. She wrote,

It's been a difficult year. My father passed away. I had surgery and a long recuperation, and someone I loved very, very much for many years has grown cold and distant. My heart has hurt so very much this year and I just couldn't seem to bounce back and get on with it.

This past Sunday was a particularly tough one for me. One of the great wants in my life has always been to have a partner in life who would go to church with me each Sunday morning. I watched my mother and father hold hands in church each Sunday, cry together, pray together . . . even after my father had his series of strokes, my mother still tenderly held his hand every Sunday morning.

Having been divorced for sixteen years, going to church by myself has often been a very lonely experience. Sunday, as I listened to your second sermon on men and women, I watched as husband after husband put his arm around his wife, or hands were being joined and I felt the tears start to run down my cheeks. That all-familiar pain was there . . . except there was something new I have never experienced in my Christian life. As clear as a bell, I heard a voice in my ear say, "I will bless you." I'm not sure how I made it home. I know I sobbed all the way there, incredulous that he touched me and that for once in my life I wasn't too busy, too distracted, or too proud to hear him.

That is the essential mission every time God's people get together — to arrange for experiences in which anyone and everyone who feels left out might hear God say, "I will bless you. You belong. This is my family, and you have a place in it." The miracle of grace is that even those of us who haven't been very consistent in sharing that message have a place, too.

QUESTIONS FOR REFLECTION AND DISCUSSION

1. What scriptural basis do you find for making the church inclusive of all persons?
2. What aspects of your congregation demonstrate the inclusiveness of the body of Christ? What aspects do not seem to do so?
3. What gifts have been given the church to help it create and maintain an inclusive fellowship?
4. Using pastor McDonald's witness as a guide, who in your congregation may have felt excluded?
5. What difference does it make that the church has frequently been more exclusive than inclusive?

CHAPTER EIGHT

Leading a Church
in the Spirit

LEADING A CHURCH in the Spirit in many ways contrasts with managing the church toward humanly conceived goals and objectives. Leadership in the Spirit emerges from the church as a spiritual organism created by Christ and infused with his presence. Christ heads up the church and provides the energy and life for those chosen to lead. Leadership, therefore, must be rooted and grounded in Christ. This rootedness in the Lord requires leaders to know him, grow up in him, and trust him as the head of the church, and the one who leads them as they lead the people of God in their mission.

Christ gives leaders to the church. Leadership is the action of authorized persons to equip, nurture, and guide a particular people of God in their mission to re-present Jesus Christ to the world. To effectively lead the church, persons in leadership roles find the source of their call and their task in a constantly growing relation to Christ himself.

I am consciously envisioning a role for leaders that contrasts sharply with the cultural church and its normal ways of leading or choosing leaders. Leadership in a Church in the Spirit cannot be by pastors who choose ministry as a career; who learn theology and the practice of ministry as a discipline; who engage in a kind of churchmanship to curry favor from church bureaucrats or church members; who treat ministry as a career path; who mouth the party line of their politically correct special interest group; who develop skills of ingratiating and manipulating to achieve personal and church goals; who seek personal advancement for salary gains and personal recognition; who long for positions of power and influence; who spend little time in cultivating their souls or enriching their minds; who are driven by external forces (with an emphasis on being driven); whose experience with the living God is shallow or nonexistent. Most of these ministers lack a vision, fear failure or job loss, and are thus frozen in mediocrity. The Church in the Spirit cannot yield to leaders who do not have an intentional, growing relationship with Jesus Christ.

The spiritual leadership being proposed also contrasts sharply with the customary criteria for choosing lay leaders. Many of our lay leaders have been chosen because of their resources, vocation, and social prominence. Often they know little of the faith beyond the oft-quoted creed; they have perverted Christian faith to legitimate their cultural values, lifestyle, and goals; they do not relate faith to their daily lives nor the world in which they work. They feel uncomfortable speaking of their faith with other Christians, and never speak to persons in their secular engagements. These compliant lay leaders give lip service to the pastor without exercising discernment; often cling to dogma in an idolatrous manner; resist change in focus, structure, and style with stubborn blindness; and sometimes threaten the withdrawal of their presence and funds if the church does not follow their demands. The Church in the Spirit cannot yield to lay leaders who neglect an intentional, growing relationship with Jesus Christ.

This analysis of perverted pastoral and lay leadership in part acknowledges my own sins, but it also offers a composite of leaders I have met in seminary students, in pastors of congregations, and in laity. I have met many of these typical leaders in courses, retreats, and conferences. I take no delight in exposing our sins, but it is imperative for us to give close attention to this issue in the church. What are the criteria for choosing leaders for a Church in the Spirit?

Leaders Are Persons in Christ

Leaders in the Church of the Spirit must be in a vital, growing relationship with Jesus Christ. This relationship consists of a new way of living, the practice of spiritual disciplines, and the expression of Christ in lifestyle decisions. A church created by the Spirit and led by the Spirit requires spiritually awakened leaders, receptive to the work of the Spirit in their lives, in the church, and in the world.

When the Rev. Don Brown went to the Trinity Episcopal Church in Sacramento he instituted a radically new posture for the church's leadership. He began with the fact that "we are the church of Jesus Christ — his body on earth." He continued: "If Christ is the head of the church, (1) we must acknowledge him as Lord, (2) submit ourselves to him, and (3) seek his guidance in what we do!"

How would we describe persons who are to give spiritual leadership? What are the characteristics of leaders who are alive in Christ? First, these leaders are called by Christ. Few, if any of them, sought the role of leader. Christ awakened a desire in them to serve and give themselves to his ministry. The call deepened as they began to discern their gifts for leading.

These gifted persons further submitted themselves to Christ. They answered the call to serve. Foundational for their ministry was their sense of call. Christ called them and they responded to him.

Leaders for Christ pray. They spend time with the Lord each day listening for his Word, wondering about the things happening in their lives, pondering the direction for the church. Their relationship grows and deepens through the time they share with him.

These leaders read the scriptures to "listen for the voice of God." The text of scripture becomes the medium that transmits the truth of God and the energy of God to them. But the scriptures also shape the mind of the leader so that she or he begins to recognize the voice of God and the ways of God.

Emphasizing the spiritual character of leaders and the skills of discernment does not establish them as holy persons over against ordinary members of the church. God calls persons to serve in leadership roles because they care about Christ, they indicate by devotion and example they are open to his guidance, and they demonstrate his gifts in their decisions. Specially called and consecrated persons do not possess holiness in themselves, but God does give them grace for deciding and guiding.

Growth must not become an obsession with the leader nor should spiritual disciplines become an end. Disciplines for growth do not deserve special merit, nor do they earn credit. These practices emerge from a posture of openness to God, faithfulness to the church, and compassion toward the world. Like all disciples, the leader constantly engages in change, ever learning new skills of leadership, a deeper sensitivity to the Spirit, and a developing loyalty to Jesus Christ as Lord.

As leaders mature they recognize that spiritual growth occurs through God's initiative and that responsive persons pay attention to God's movement in their lives. The way of God not only comes through prayer, worship, and scripture, but in the ordinary events of our lives — in the persons we meet, the thoughts we think, and the opportunities that open to us. The growing leader must learn to be relaxed, perceptive, aware, and responsive to the work of God in his or her life.

Spiritual Leaders Are Christ-Directed

Spiritual leaders in Christ's church live with the question, "What is Christ calling this community to be and do?" They listen for the answer to this question in text, context, fellowship, and the larger world. They especially attend the call of God in human pain, whether caused by ignorance, disaster, oppression, or injustice. Because Christ directs the church, it must never substitute its own will for his; it must turn to him, listen to him, and make decisions with the conviction that Christ himself leads them. Leaders who help a congregation decide on its mission will empower the people to act in response to Christ. A response to the call of Christ transforms "church work" into ministry and mission in obedience to Christ. This shift releases motivation, generates power, and inspires sacrifice. Furthermore, ministry in response to Christ sanctifies the work and makes it a medium for communion with Christ.

As spiritual leaders seek to discern God's will, they look to persons inside and outside the church for clues about Christ's agenda for the church. Persons beyond the membership present the church with pain, hunger, and hopelessness. They provide the church with the shape of its mission. But persons inside the church, by their affirmation of their leaders' decisions, give them confirmation and spiritual support. Their affirmation comes not only in words of approval but in obedient response to the call of Christ to participate in the mission. The response to the call has its grounding in the gifts of the people of God. The picture seems complete. God calls to the church through human need; the caring hearts and minds of spiritual leaders respond to it with discernment and action.

This way of leading suggests that hearing Christ's call constitutes mission. The call and the mission are not born in the boardroom out of the good intentions of benevolent leaders, but in the upper room where leaders pray and wait for God to speak. When leaders make decisions in response to the call of God, mission has a spiritual quality marked by urgency and immediacy.

The call of Christ does not ignore the feelings, values, and needs of others but neither does it yield to social or political or financial pressure. In many instances this will set the church over against the prevailing cultural norms; it will make Christians odd and peculiar; following Christ will sometimes evoke harsh criticism and judgment. Persecution should not seem strange to a people who follow the crucified One. Christian faithfulness requires taking daring risks in love.

The call of Christ empowers for ministry. To be called and sent embodies in the baptized the authority of the one who calls and sends. "As the Father has sent me, so send I you." The church, sent into the world by Christ, goes into the world with the authority of Christ. Sharing in the mission of Christ in a particular place in response to a particular need has the power of God behind it. This mission does not belong to the church; it is Christ's. Those responding to his call can be assured that he is with them, that he works through them, that he does his work in the world through them. What a contrast with asking him to bless the plans we have made.

Capacity to Create Community

The leader of the Spirit-empowered church must have the capacity to evoke and nurture community. Even though spiritual community is not a human creation, leaders can set the stage for it to be born, or they can undermine existing community by creating conditions hostile to it. As we have seen, community refers to participation in a vision that transcends the individual in the church, but it also denotes the interpersonal relations within the church. A minimum requirement for leaders is that they know and be able to articulate the vision of the particular church and have the relational skills to create and maintain relationships with members of the church. Because of the critical nature of community for the mission of the church, leaders must have both visionary and relational skills in order to be generative leaders.

If the church is the community of Christ, his earthly form, then the community draws its life from Christ. Those who guide fill a major role by helping members, and groups of members, realize their relation to Christ. The development of the Christ life within the membership manifests itself in many forms: teaching, fellowship, spiritual direction, sharing in mission — to name a few. Once again, the leader's task of helping members grow up in Christ illustrates the dependence of the church upon Christ.

For the church to be inclusive of all persons and cultures, it must find its unity in Christ and not in cultural conventions. To avoid factions and the "issue agenda," all of us must keep the focus on the unity of life in Christ.

The Leader as Vision Caster

A leader in the Church of the Spirit must be a vision caster, one who lives the vision and holds it before the eyes of the congregation. Vision relates the church to the future; it visualizes how things might be. The wings of a vision are broad and long, casting a huge shadow that embraces a diverse number of persons. It is amorphous, open, and flexible, and it permits easy entrance and embrace; it is soft and malleable, capable of being formed and reformed. To cast a vision, leaders need a future orientation, a *positive* future orientation — a picture so grand that it cannot be accomplished without the grace and power of God.

The bearers and proclaimers of a vision generally see the goal more clearly than the strategy for getting there. These vision casters have the power to arouse enthusiasm and stir the excitement that energizes a congregation. Some approaches toward realizing the vision may, at first, appear to be contradictory. The lack of exactness opens the door for all persons to respond to the initial vision, to add their insights and shape it according to their gifts and dreams. The mechanics of realizing a vision and the pitfalls that lie in the way must be dealt with, but they are not the first matters of importance for the vision caster and the visioning congregation.

After the work of visioning and the discernment of new directions, the call of Christ requires spokespersons. The visionary by this time no longer articulates his or her vision. The original vision has been shaped and reshaped by the prayers, responses, and guidance of the congregation so that it has become the vision of the whole community. The heads of the congregation keep the goal fresh by reporting on developments, evaluating progress, and working through conflicts. Visionary leadership provides guidance in evaluating programs, in ministries and style, and in the actualization of the vision.

A vision possesses characteristics of metaphor, parable, and story. Its narrative quality makes it flexible and subject to change, but the aim remains constant. The vision usually can be reduced to a dozen or so words. It permeates every serious gathering of the community and serves as the norm for their life and mission.

The Sources of Visions

The vision has its grounding in Christ, informed by the context, inspired by the Spirit, and shaped by the gifts in the community. Ultimately, all visions must originate in Christ who is the foundation of the church. Vision is, therefore, the effort of the church to imagine the will of God in its particular place of ministry.

The way of the vision usually has tinges of mystery around it, and this mystery resides in the mysterious work of Christ. If there is no living Christ, there is no vision. But he does touch blind eyes causing them to see; he anoints the eyes of the heart and gives spiritual vision. True vision always comes from him. When Christ gives a vision it is always gratuitous; we do not earn it or merit it. The vision comes with a sudden but vague burst of energy that gradually grows and takes on concreteness. Vision comes unexpectedly — like a flash of light. It explodes into a motivation that has elements of conviction, joy and delight, energy to act, and courage to fail. All these subjective aspects of vision I take to be the influence of the Holy Spirit acting upon the human spirit or human consciousness.

Most aspects of a vision we recognize in Jesus' healing of the blind man — his cry for help, getting Jesus' attention, a free touch, the miracle of sight, the burst of praise and the sight restored. When a vision comes to a community it is often in response to a cry for help, to which Jesus responds through our hands and feet. He freely touches the eyes of their hearts and holds a vision before them so that they see their mission and delight in him who ministers through them.

At the beginning, the vision usually occurs in one person, not in the whole group. But when this person shares the vision, others affirm, correct, and enlarge it. In this way they become participants in the vision. The most logical person to share the vision with acknowledged leaders is the person to whom it has been given.

With respect to the vision-casting quality of leaders, other considerations should claim our attention. The pastor, for example, may not be a visionary and thus must look to the gifts of others to fill this need. The pastor surely will pray for them and trust their guidance. The pastor can embrace and proclaim their vision, making it accessible for the whole body of Christ.

If the pastor does not have a vision or embrace and proclaim the vision shared by others, the church cannot be driven by a vision. Most likely this church will fix its attention on the past, defend the status quo, become blind to changes in its context and back its way into the future. Reality for this visionless church lies in the past, and it will soon die because it has no idea where it is going.

124

A vision costs a congregation faithfulness, commitment, and often sacrifice. Just as a vision unifies and focuses the congregation, it also places a demand upon the bearers of the vision. These visionaries become single-minded in their pursuit of the call. It consumes their waking thoughts, their time and energy, and drives them toward their dreams. Ministry with a vision is an incomparable experience; it is the difference between doing church work and participating in the ministry of Christ.

Leaders Are Discerners of the Spirit

Leaders in the Church of the Spirit must be discerners of the Spirit and of spirits. We have emphasized repeatedly that the invisible, ever present Christ constitutes the church's life and ministry. The communication of his life to the body presents itself in the Word, by the Spirit, in history or through persons. Most often he communicates by indirection by wearing many guises. On one occasion he comes as a word, on another as a text, at times in the gifts and interests of his people, and often in the larger issues of society. He comes, speaks, and acts, but is received only by those who are prepared to welcome him! This subtlety forces us to be awake and aware.

The issue of proper discernment always gnaws at the soul of leaders. "How do we distinguish between Christ and our own unconscious longings? How do we know that the vision of the ministry comes from Christ?" These questions of discernment require us to be familiar with all the rules of discernment so that we may rightly judge.

In this discussion of leadership in the spiritually alive congregation, we have emphasized a different image of leadership in both the pastor and lay leaders. The emphasis has fallen upon the reality of the living Christ in the community, guiding his church in mission. To discern this guidance the leader must be a spiritually alive person, growing in the faith. When we begin to select and equip leaders who are growing in their faith and developing clearer discernment, the church will be transformed for Christ's mission.

A Corroborative Witness

My home state of Indiana may not be a paradise for those who like to surf, ski, or climb mountains, but it's a very special place for those who enjoy spelunking. That's caving — self-guided exploration of the muck, mire, and wonder of a limestone cavern. Spelunking has been on my list of fun things to do for more than a quarter century. I'm no vertical caver — one of those acrobats who moves up and down a wall with sure hands or rappelling equipment. I prefer horizontal motion: moving in and out of bedrock sieves, splashing through water, checking out crevices and formations along the way.

I'm also the first to admit that there are limits to what I'm willing to do in a cave. Over the course of several years I had made half a dozen visits to a particular cavern near Bedford, Indiana, always halting at a very low and narrow place. At this juncture the ceiling comes down and almost meets the surface of very cold water. The only way through this pinch-point is to remove your helmet, tip your head sideways, ease into that freezing groundwater, keep your mouth near the rock ceiling for gulps of air, then crawl on an elbow for thirty or forty feet in darkness. Half a dozen times I took a long look, stretched, pronounced the cave trip a great success, and turned back.

A few summers ago I finally did it. I took the plunge and went through the "narrow gate," the harrowing spot that had always intimidated me and kept me from exploring the rest of the cave. I went because I trusted the word of spelunking friends who assured me there really was a dry place just out of sight beyond the water. And in my wake came three other friends who said, "If *Glenn* can do it, it can't be that bad."

The congregation of the twenty-first century will face countless pinch-points — ministry moments when the way forward seems blocked and the assembly is only too happy to conclude that it's been a wonderful trip, so why don't we just stop right here. Leadership is finding a way through the narrow places and inviting others to follow so that the people of God might explore the wonder of the future they are being offered as a gift.

By that definition a leader is one who concludes, *I must go first.* I

126

entered ministry trained and motivated to teach. I was prepared to inculcate principles of spiritual living — in the classroom, in sermons, in conversation. This teacher, however, turned out to be a slow learner. Years passed before I heard what a few people were articulating ("Show me how to do that") and what almost everyone else was silently thinking ("That's a nice principle that I'll never attempt until I see somebody I know actually doing it").

My preaching about the value of small groups had little impact until I publicly witnessed to my *participating* in a small group. Verbal challenges to financial sacrifice would occasionally stir people to discussion, but the Sunday morning I itemized what the McDonalds planned to give to a capital campaign, and described in detail the process we used in our decision making, actually stirred families to *action*. For years my instruction concerning the discipline of prayer was impotent, since thoughtful listeners could tell I didn't pray. Sharing the struggles and victories of a halting new prayer life immediately helped raise the prayer temperature throughout the congregation. Leaders go first. God's people imitate what they see trusted leaders doing.

A few years ago an 84-year-old woman who lives in our county was shopping at a mall. As she made her way back toward her car in the parking lot she was terrified to see two strange teenage boys sitting in her front seat. They had cranked up the stereo and were rocking away without a care in the world. Electing not to shout for help, the woman reached into her purse and pulled out a handgun. She opened the driver's side door and pointed the gun right at the teenagers and said, "You get out of this car right now, and I don't want to see you stop running!" The boys, badly shaken, exited as quickly as they could. Recovering her composure, the woman settled in behind the wheel and inserted her car key. It didn't work. *The car belonged to the boys.*

Just when I'm poised to muscle my way to the front of the crowd, making threats and shouting, "I'm your leader, so here's the way it's going to be!," I am reminded that Jesus did not overcome the world with a show of power. His spiritual leadership was authenticated by a quiet demonstration of trust in the Father. A leader's quiet and non-anxious presence is often the greatest demonstration of authority.

Leaders must also *share with someone else what they know.* That means mentoring. When the congregation voted to approve a five-year emphasis on mentoring as part of a larger strategic plan, I wondered how such a helpful but fuzzy idea could ever be implemented. Three lay "champions" and a staff person became a team that made it happen.

They began with education — creative, continuing, redundant teaching in every ministry corner of the church. They patiently made a case that learning a leadership skill or developing a creative ministry and failing to pass the torch to the next generation is a spiritual catastrophe. By age 33 Alexander the Great had pasted together an ancient world empire as broad as the United States is long. He had fabulous plans for further conquests, but a malaria-toting mosquito got in his way. Alexander died with no heir to his empire and no designated successor. Within twelve years virtually everything he had worked for had disintegrated.

It could have been different. Long before malaria picked him off, Alexander could have chosen to die in a different way, by being willing to "die" to the part of his dream that required him to be in charge of everything. If he had mentored his vision to others along the way, and shared with them the opportunity to help manage the dream, his empire might have lasted for centuries.

Our church cannot afford an Alexander the Great. *The development of new, rising leaders is more important than building private kingdoms.* The mentor team introduced a plan by which seasoned elders help newly elected elders get their sea legs. Retiring deacons take six months to coach their successors. Youth ministry team members pour their lives into teenagers who are seeking discipleship. Mature high school teens mentor middle schoolers. In a ministry called "Heart to Heart" two dozen spiritually mature women each spend a year in conversation, friendship, and spiritual life sharing with one other woman who is eager to grow in Christ. Each Sunday school class is directed by a team that includes a lead teacher and several assistants who are apprenticed as learners for at least one year. Increasingly our leadership community is reminded, "If God is showing you something, who are you showing in return? Multiply the gift!"

Leaders of a Church in the Spirit must also choose to *be accountable to other leaders.* The community is healthy when its leaders are in healthy community with God and with each other. To be a small group or ministry leader means to enter a relationship with a lay or pastoral coach. The coach arranges regular meetings in which to listen, encourage, and advise the leaders under his or her care (usually no more than five or six), and to watch each leader's heart monitor for God.

One legacy of the North American church is its continuing malpractice in the care and handling of one of its most treasured resources: lay women and men who are willing to serve others for the sake of Jesus Christ. The degree to which we have allowed God's people to overfunction and to forsake a lifestyle of spending sufficient time in God's presence is shameful indeed. Thus we attempt to say loudly and clearly at the beginning of every coaching relationship: Accountability to another leader is not a subtle form of control, but a special, personal safeguard against a multitude of spiritual breakdowns.

Accountability has become a weekly exercise for the pastoral staff. One hour each Wednesday morning we set aside time for open-hearted sharing around a series of personal questions. We have chosen to meet in two groups, one for women staff members and one for men. I've talked with other pastors who have questioned this separation, but my experience (at least from a male perspective) is that the arrangement permits profoundly more intimate sharing concerning thought life and personal behaviors that are too crucial *not* to talk about. Our questions include:

- Did I spend significant time this week in personal prayer and worship of God?
- Did I take time to study?
- Was I with my spouse and children this week so that *they* would say I truly spent quality time with them?
- Did I invest time in the lay leaders for whom I am responsible?
- Did I spend time inappropriately with a member of the opposite sex?
- Was my thought life and fantasy life a reflection of the holiness of God?
- Did I speak the truth this week? Was my tongue flippant or wounding?

- Did I make financial decisions consistent with my commitment to Christ and his mission?
- What does God seem to be teaching me this week?

When our regular staff meeting begins during the hour that follows, we commence with "Winners of the Week." Staff members cite any and every happening of the previous seven days that deserves applause and thanks to God. I am always stunned by the stories of creative lay leaders, children with outrageously bold ideas, saints who rush in at just the right moment to help the office dispatch a mailing, prayers answered and spiritual directions discerned. Leader-to-leader accountability includes the necessity of lifting each other up with the accounts of the Spirit's deeds in our midst. More than anything else, these stories stoke our fires and keep them blazing.

A final word about the cave. I wouldn't even have attempted the narrow place had I not known trusted people had gone there before me. God's path into the future will always feature pinch-points. The gift of leadership means instilling in the next generation a confidence that we can go through the narrow gate together.

QUESTIONS FOR REFLECTION AND DISCUSSION

1. Compare the character of leaders in your church with leaders in the cultural church.
2. What spiritual characteristics do you expect in your leaders?
3. Who are the vision casters in your congregation? How are they treated?
4. What aspects of Pastor McDonald's leadership perspective challenge you?
5. What changes would be appropriate for your church to make in the selection, training, and support of leaders?

CHAPTER NINE

Teaching in a Church
in the Spirit

SINCE WE HAVE chosen Jesus, the Christ, as a paradigm for the church, it is imperative that we consider the church as a Teacher. Jesus devoted a major portion of his ministry to teaching. Fifteen times in the Gospels and once in the Acts of the Apostles the text indicates that Jesus taught his disciples about the kingdom of God and the manner of their lives. To count the number of times the words "teach" or "taught" appear in the text does not exhaust Jesus' efforts to inform his followers. He taught them mostly by his example, and by inviting them to engage in the mission. As we have suggested, his whole ministry focused on preparing his followers to continue his mission in the world. Because of Jesus' emphasis on teaching, the Church in the Spirit must recover teaching the faith and nurturing disciples for a life of missionary engagement.

Jesus the Teacher

A complete investigation of the content and style of Jesus' teaching would be more exhaustive than our purpose calls for, but we will examine the role of teaching in Jesus' ministry and several illustrations of his style and content. Our aim is to challenge the congregation to re-think its goals, methods, and content in teaching.

Jesus primarily addressed himself to the training of his followers. He called a few disciples from Galilee to follow him. They left their nets, homes, and security to follow this itinerant evangelist. According to Mark's narrative of the call, their earliest experience consisted in receiving his teaching.

> As he went a little farther, he saw James son of Zebedee and his brother John, who were in their boat mending the nets. Immediately he called them; and they left their father Zebedee in the boat with the hired men, and followed him. They went to Capernaum; and when the sabbath came, he entered the synagogue and taught. They were astounded at his teaching, for he taught them as one having authority, and not as the scribes. (Mark 1:19-22)

Jesus taught both his disciples and the crowds with his own authority. His teaching had a convictional quality that sprang from his own being, and not conferred by the rabbis. He taught them without quoting first one rabbi and then another. His authority sprang from another source.

Jesus instructed his followers about the life that brings fulfillment. His instruction on the mount explained to them the values of the kingdom, the attitudes they should have about common experiences in life, and their role like salt, light, and leaven in spreading the kingdom.

> When Jesus saw the crowds, he went up the mountain; and after he sat down, his disciples came to him. Then he began to speak, and taught them, saying:
> "Blessed are the poor in spirit, for theirs is the kingdom of heaven.
> "Blessed are those who mourn, for they will be comforted.
> "Blessed are the meek, for they will inherit the earth.
> "Blessed are those who hunger and thirst for righteousness, for they will be filled.
> "Blessed are the merciful, for they will receive mercy.

"Blessed are the pure in heart, for they will see God.

"Blessed are the peacemakers, for they will be called children of God.

"Blessed are those who are persecuted for righteousness' sake, for theirs is the kingdom of heaven.

"Blessed are you when people revile you and persecute you and utter all kinds of evil against you falsely on my account. Rejoice and be glad, for your reward is great in heaven, for in the same way they persecuted the prophets who were before you.

"You are the salt of the earth; but if salt has lost its taste, how can its saltiness be restored? It is no longer good for anything, but is thrown out and trampled under foot.

"You are the light of the world. A city built on a hill cannot be hid. No one after lighting a lamp puts it under the bushel basket, but on the lampstand, and it gives light to all in the house. In the same way, let your light shine before others, so that they may see your good works and give glory to your Father in heaven." (Matt. 5:1-16)

Note how Jesus used visual images couched in terse phrases that addressed the experience of his listeners. This teaching style resonates with the wisdom tradition in Job, Proverbs, and the Song of Songs. He does not explain his metaphors but sends his followers away to wonder about the meaning of "being salt or light or leaven." His teaching has a strange, provocative power that teases the imagination into seeking truth.

Jesus voluntarily taught the principles of the kingdom; but regarding prayer, he awaited their request for instruction. When the request came, it brought an immediate response. Perhaps Jesus' rigorous practice of prayer compelled them to ask for instruction. Maybe the disciples were jealous of John's disciples, who had already been instructed. Whatever the reason, they somehow developed a yearning to learn from the Master.

He was praying in a certain place, and after he had finished, one of his disciples said to him, "Lord, teach us to pray, as John taught his disciples." He said to them, "When you pray, say:

Father, hallowed be your name.
Your kingdom come.
Give us each day our daily bread.
And forgive us our sins,
    for we ourselves forgive everyone indebted to us.
And do not bring us to the time of trial."

And he said to them, "Suppose one of you has a friend, and you go to him at midnight and say to him, 'Friend, lend me three loaves of bread; for a friend of mine has arrived, and I have nothing to set before him.' And he answers from within, 'Do not bother me; the door has already been locked, and my children are with me in bed; I cannot get up and give you anything.' I tell you, even though he will not get up and give him anything because he is his friend, at least because of his persistence he will get up and give him whatever he needs.

"So I say to you, Ask, and it will be given you; search, and you will find; knock, and the door will be opened for you. For everyone who asks receives, and everyone who searches finds, and for everyone who knocks, the door will be opened. Is there anyone among you who, if your child asks for a fish, will give a snake instead of a fish? Or if the child asks for an egg, will give a scorpion? If you then, who are evil, know how to give good gifts to your children, how much more will the heavenly Father give the Holy Spirit to those who ask him!" (Luke 11:1-13)

In this teaching session Jesus gave to his followers the prayer that the faithful have prayed for nearly 2,000 years. According to John Calvin, it is the perfect prayer; nothing has been omitted. Jesus' way of prayer centers in God — God's name, God's kingdom, God's will. Jesus also placed human need at the opposite pole — daily bread, forgiveness of sin, deliverance from evil's power. He taught his disciples to honor God and to fulfill their lives for the glory of God. According to Jesus' instruction, these polarities remain in dynamic tension.

Jesus also taught the importance of persistence in prayer. We are to continually ask of God the good things that we need. Like a woman going to her neighbor to borrow food to feed a guest, we keep asking until we receive the answers we seek. Our persistence does not persuade a reluctant God as much as it clarifies our own desires. Notice how Jesus uses a brief vignette filled with images to communicate an array of insights. Unexpected events occur like an unannounced visitor; the visitor threatens to embarrass the host because she could not show proper hospitality. Recalling that her neighbor may have extra bread, she dashes out the back door and goes to this neighbor. She raps on the door, but the neighbor urges her to go away. But she will not leave without bread and risks offending the neighbor by continuing to knock. Persistence pays off; she gets the bread, and she serves the bread to her visitor.

Jesus told this story to invite us into the delicate world of divine/human transactions. Prayer to God is somehow like getting bread from a reluctant neighbor to feed an unexpected guest. It takes a certain tenacity to pray aright. Interestingly, Jesus did not explain the story but left the interpretation to his listeners' imagination. Perhaps this is an important aspect of his methodology, especially for a culture that must make everything perfectly clear.

The Church as Teacher

Imagining the church as a corporate expression of Jesus Christ includes seeing the church as a teacher of Truth. For the church to re-present Christ in the twenty-first century, it must rethink the goals, methods, and content of its teaching ministry. To become an authentic expression of "Jesus, the teacher," the Church in the Spirit will also develop an appropriate teaching style that communicates the vitality of the faith.

Obviously, the old model of teaching used in forming the boomers failed. It failed because it did not do what good teaching does — initiate persons into the experience of the Spirit and the kingdom and form them in Christ. Spiritual formation in Christ is the educational task of the church, not merely the passing on of information about the faith.

The instructional issue is clear: How does the living Christ take up residence in, grow toward maturity in, and actualize the kingdom of God through the members of his body? The efforts to imagine new ways of initiation into the body of Christ provide goals for the instructional enterprise; teaching aims to provide the content, environment, and experience that will help the baptized learn how to practice the faith in their daily lives. In addition to what has been said about the tasks of initiation, we find it necessary now to explore the components, methods, and models of formation.

Formation

While writing these pages I participated in a spirituality group, gathered from across the United States, representing various faith orientations. Those who planned the conference hoped for a fruitful interchange from a multicultural group. As a way of bringing focus to the discussion, they chose the topic of formation.

As you might expect, formation evoked a variety of feelings and judgments. One contingent held that formation of others was impossible. Another judged formation to be an imposing of alien ideas and values on others. Still another group resisted the notion of formation because it seemed to hint of manipulation. This experience made clear to me that I cannot assume my idea of formation matches yours.

By formation in Christ, I do not mean that a clearly defined pattern exists for shaping every person in the faith. To make this assumption would deny the uniqueness of individuals — their history, context, and stage of maturity. Formation takes these factors seriously and engages persons in ways appropriate for their development as disciples of Jesus Christ. To fail in this response to the rich diversity of persons in the body of Christ would leave no option but to manipulate everyone into conformity with a pre-established pattern. Although manipulation often occurs in the name of "formation," it certainly falls short of Christ's own model. Clearly, formation does not mean adopting subtle manipulative procedures administered by the expert to properly shape persons according to another's design.

Formation does not imply that the teacher knows what the student should become and can thus proceed confidently towards the goal. This perversion occurs when the teacher assumes that he is wise and the student is ignorant, and that formation consists of the wise teacher sharing knowledge with the ignorant student.

While the teacher may have information that the student does not possess, she also learns with the student. The person effective in formation presupposes that God has a purpose that will become clearer through growth and development. In formation, the teacher explores new challenges and insights with the student, and becomes a learner *with* the student. In this give and take of information in a trusting relationship, both the teacher and the student are formed. All healthy, effective teaching leads to mutual formation.

While the teacher does not have a blueprint for achieving it, the goal of formation in Christ guides her choices and responses. Being conformed to Christ opens up the possibility for great diversity.

We have been created in the image of God, yet each person is unique. All persons have different gifts, a variety of potentialities, and contrasting life-shaping experiences. The expressions of conformity to Christ will be as different as all these formative elements in our lives. Perhaps our conformity to Christ is not so much imitating the example of Jesus as being conformed to the person we were created to be. When we understand conformity as becoming true to our created self, formation means becoming what we are essentially, rather than denying our uniqueness to become someone else. The peculiar uniqueness of God's creative excellence demands that each person be taken seriously.

The formation of the individual member of the body of Christ begins with a focus on the uniqueness of each person, but continued formation requires knowledge of the faith. Without knowing about Jesus Christ, how can there be conformity to Christ? Therefore, the story of the faith funds the imagination of those being formed. Surely the story will include the annunciation, birth, baptism, and teachings of Jesus. Without these data about Jesus, life-shaping decisions will be impossible. But formation requires more than passing on information. To be effective, these data about Christ will be received best in a community of loving fellowship.

Formation in Christ prepares persons to participate fully in the Church in the Spirit. The changes our vision calls for can only become a reality when members of the body of Christ have been prepared and equipped spiritually to participate in the new reality. As we have suggested, this spiritual formation begins with a vital community of faith. And it expands with authentic initiation into this community, participating in the mission of the community, discerning the call of God, and learning to pray and worship.

Formation is one of the church's never-ending tasks. Members change, circumstances change, the Spirit moves in new ways, and these realities demand continuous adaptation. At every juncture in life persons are confronted with challenges, new opportunities to understand the faith and appropriate it in greater depth. Without a caring, supportive community, persons either fall by the wayside or they quietly suffer in loneliness that leads to despair. The Church alive in the Spirit will work seriously at the task of forming its membership.

Teaching the Teacher in Formation

All that has been set forth about initiation applies to teachers of the faith. For teaching to be effective, it must be done by persons growing in their knowledge of Christ and concerned about others' spiritual development. The effective teacher in the Church in the Spirit teaches from a sense of call. Because the body of Christ receives its ultimate authority from Christ who lives in its midst, the Lord himself calls teachers of the faith. Those who teach with a sense of call not only have commitment, they teach with an authority and freedom that is contagious. To staff the church with teachers called by Christ, the church will provide settings in which they can discern their gift of teaching and hear their call to ministry.

The teacher's call has its foundation in the gifts of Christ to his body. He has given to the church "teachers."

Therefore it is said, "When he ascended on high he made captivity itself a captive; he gave gifts to his people." (When it says, "He as-

138

cended," what does it mean but that he had also descended into the lower parts of the earth? He who descended is the same one who ascended far above all the heavens, so that he might fill all things.) The gifts he gave were that some would be apostles, some prophets, some evangelists, some pastors and teachers, to equip the saints for the work of ministry, for building up the body of Christ, until all of us come to the unity of the faith and of the knowledge of the Son of God, to maturity, to the measure of the full stature of Christ. (Eph. 4:8-13)

The teacher functions, then, not only from an immediate sense of calling to a particular task, but receives empowerment from the teaching office given by Christ.

Among those called to the office of teacher there are varieties of gifts and these different gifts combine in complementary ways to express the will of Christ. Some teachers bring the gift of imagination, others creativity, still others discernment, while many bring basic data of the faith. This variety joins together in teaching the body of Christ as it grows toward maturity.

Whatever the subject, instructors in the Church of the Spirit possess one clear focus that conditions every endeavor. Teaching aims to form every member in the body according to the person's gifts, call, and uniqueness. This aim can be realized only where teachers point every member of the body of Christ to the cosmic Christ. He is the ground and aim of their teaching; and when teachers succeed in this task, Christ draws persons to himself and forms them for their own fulfillment and ministry.

Instruction not only forms persons in Christ, it also awakens them to the reality of his living presence. As disciples mature and the Spirit awakens in them an awareness of Christ's living presence, spiritually sensitive teachers help them discern his voice. The task of discernment challenges all teachers, whether clergy or lay, to attend to their own growth. Their effectiveness as guides to others depends upon a growing sensitivity to Christ's presence in their own lives. As their awareness expands, they will become more adept at recognizing, naming, and responding to the presence of the risen and living Lord in their own lives. And, as they develop in their own faith, they will become more helpful to disciples engaged in their process of discernment.

Growth in awareness of God's presence in our lives, responsiveness to the communication of God, and service to Christ deepen and mature faith. Life in Christ becomes a dialogue in which both persons and congregations discern the mind of Christ and respond to his call. Dialogical living fills our lives with challenge and excitement. The circumstances of our lives constantly present new data for discernment and the dilemma of what God is seeking to communicate to us drives us to Christ. Listening and responding to Christ in each new context takes on a narrative character in our memory and shapes our lives. The substance of this dialogue, begun in our particular situation and responded to out of our discernment, becomes a part of our remembered narrative. These experiences of Christ provide a foundation for our action and the framework for further discernment.

Methods of Instruction

Since our intention is to explore the spirituality of teaching, we will not offer an exhaustive list of teaching methodologies but will aim to be illustrative in both method and goal. We want to suggest several means at the disposal of the teacher to evoke, mediate, and form Christ in the life of the individual and in the corporate community. An exhaustive discussion of pedagogical method would take us beyond our purpose. We will, however, illustrate how the spiritual aim of the teacher affects the use of particular methods.

In the task of formation nothing ranks higher in effectiveness than the community itself; life in the community exerts the greatest power of formation. The faith community teaches persons a language, a worldview, an identity, and goals. Life in the community provides support for the plausibility structures undergirding these formative elements. Because of this crucial role of the vital community, efforts to strengthen the fellowship will never be wasted.

Words have enormous power to create, form, transform, and direct. Words like Christ, Son of God, salvation, and forgiveness create images with which to imagine the world of everyday experience. Words like love, obedience, and patience suggest ways to live our lives. Trust, believe, receive are words that tell us how to interact with the data of our lives; these words not only create images, they also evoke actions and shape attitudes.

Spoken words have enormous power to form and transform the life and vision of both the individual and the community. Because words provide a way to name and understand, without them there is no meaningful experience. Experiences like an encounter with Christ, a deep sense of guidance, a witness to the closeness of God, when named, can be remembered and connected to our story of faith. If we cannot name those experiences, they slip away like forgotten dreams. When through words our experiences become connected to our lives, they form our identity and values. Words joined with reason permit us to recall experiences, relate them to new situations, edit them, and even reinterpret them. In a similar way words have a role in the collective memory of the congregation, helping it discern God's guidance. Teaching in the church helps us learn the language of faith and interpret this language in the light of God's revelation in our world today.

This emphasis on "words" as vehicles of instruction may seem quite obvious. My intention in discussing "words" as a method of instruction underscores our need for a common vocabulary to name the action of God among us and to interpret this action in our ongoing life together. At the same time that I emphasize the power and value of words, I am very clear that the transmission of the Spirit cannot be communicated through words alone but requires the Spirit's action. Words without the Spirit are dead, and dead words cannot create or sustain life. While I realize God can speak in unrestricted ways, it seems that persons in whom the words of faith have been incarnate speak these words with life-giving authority.

Words communicate data, but parables have a power to evoke experiences beyond flat speech. Parables are word pictures that subvert our common way of seeing and disorient us to the point that we are driven to look again at matters seemingly settled. This unsettling of the hearer creates an opening for reevaluation, for new decisions, and for change. Parables are like metaphors; they grasp reality with a grip

141

forbidden to linear logic. Parables apprehend more than we can draw out of them in words, and they resist all analysis that would take them apart to examine their individual pieces. Parables often contain precise images and narrative details but signify a reality beyond both.

Parables teach by indirection. As an example, look at the story of the Good Samaritan. A lawyer asks, "Who is my neighbor?" Jesus very easily could have answered, "A neighbor is one who befriends others in need regardless of race, religion, culture, or economic position." But he chose to answer in another manner, a story about an outcast who was beaten and robbed and left to die. In the story, several religious persons passed him by, but when a Samaritan came along the road, he saw the poor man's plight and offered care.

Notice how this story does not directly answer the question asked by the lawyer. The story contains the answer but the inquirer must enter into the story; he must transform the narrative into an existential answer to his question. The lawyer cannot reflect on the issue isolated from his feelings and values. The parable has these multiple dimensions that communicate and transform by indirection.

In another parable, the "Pearl of Great Price," a man finds a jewel and sells all to possess it. The surface meaning suggests the jewel meets the needs of the one who possesses it — security, self-esteem, well-being. The jewel is a treasure to show friends who will praise the owner and will wonder about his grand treasure. The jewel evokes amazement, like the magic of Aladdin's lamp or the genie in the magic bottle.

But at a deeper level this parable is not about drawing attention to wealth or gaining praise or even security; it points to sacrificing everything for the one thing worth your whole life. Devotion to God ranks highest among all our commitments, but does surrendering everything for the love of God exhaust the meaning of this brief story?

Stories like these help the teacher communicate the Christ life to persons without tying it up with cords of dogma. Parables are mysterious stories with hidden depths, whose plots shift because they are clothed in mystery. The parable of the Good Samaritan seems to stand halfway between parable and story. It does not purport to report facts; it is presumably a fictional narrative that answers the lawyer's question, and more. But these symbolic stories of Jesus make their greatest impact when told to a community that has been shaped by testimony, like Peter's experience in Joppa and the coming of the Spirit in Jerusalem. A rehearsal of testimony to these events carried theological freight as rich as the parables.

The church remembered and retold Peter's story about the rooftop experience in Joppa, when the sheet was lowered from heaven filled with unclean animals and he was commanded to kill and eat. This incident, recorded in the memory of the early church, was neither parable nor dogma but testimony to an event in the life of Peter that carried heavy theological freight. This testimony held numerous implications for the gospel, the mission of the young church, and the relation of Jews and Gentiles. It helped them answer questions like: How do Christians relate to the Jewish purity laws? Are non-Jews included in the covenant of Christ? Does Christ still speak to us since his death? What is the risk of obedience to him? Peter's experience in Joppa offers an answer to each of these questions.

The coming of the Spirit at Pentecost and Paul's conversion on the road to Damascus relate encounters with the risen Christ similar to Peter's rooftop revelation. Each of these Pauline testimonies points the way for the early church in the manner of Peter's vision on the roof in Joppa. These experiences with Christ, related as testimony, open up the reality of the gospel and mediate the Spirit to the hearers. The effective teacher has the stories of both the Old and New Testaments to use as "moving metaphors" or "active similes" to communicate the Spirit. These narratives demonstrate transformative power by drawing the listener into a consciousness of the presence of Christ and funding the imagination with gospel material. The teacher as a witness draws the mind of the listener into Christ's presence. Both the teacher and the testimony serve as a medium to transmit Christ's presence and healing.

Teaching with biblical testimony, stories, and parables often leads to instruction through contemporary parables and current witness. Though the biblical models are always normative, the Spirit cannot be bound so tightly by these narratives that current revelation is denied. The Spirit still inspires new parables in the teacher's mind, and works in our ordinary lives creating current testimony. Creative teachers maintain a receptivity to the Spirit's in-breaking and the creation of new forms for old truths.

Another dynamic medium for instruction rests in the relationship between the teacher and her students. The teacher's knowledge of the subject and of her own person provides material for teaching. The teacher always teaches out of her being, who she is. The teacher's relation with the student provides connectors, like phone lines or radio waves, through which both information and the presence of Christ pass. In this knowing and loving relationship, the presence of Christ in the teacher evokes the image, and transformation occurs through this encounter.

In this exploration of the teaching role of the church, I have grounded the church's ministry in Jesus the teacher. Because he taught about God, the church teaches. As he taught through actions as well as words, the whole life of the church serves the teaching function. Following Jesus, the church uses words to communicate the message, but words without the Spirit cannot transform lives. Like Christ, the church turns to parable, narrative, and testimony to open space for the creative imagination to connect with the Spirit. Parable, testimony, and narrative prove good companions of the Spirit. Finally, the church's teaching aims at the formation of disciples; if it fails at this task, its teaching has been for naught.

A Corroborative Witness

When we organized a ten-week Wednesday-evening class and christened it "God for Dummies" — hoping to accomplish for theology what the popular book series had done for thorny subjects like computers and taxes — I wondered who in the world might show up. The thirty-two people who materialized one night had little in common. There were new members and pioneer members; inquisitive X-ers who rarely attended church and senior-age couples who were worshiping before I was born; some who brought leather-bound Bibles and others who came with empty hands. Their single commonality was a striking one: All were willing to publicly present themselves as "dummies" when it came to the most basic Christian teachings about God.

For a decade and a half our congregation has been on a steep learning curve regarding how its members are learning . . . or not learning. It wasn't long ago that church leaders in North America could safely make three assumptions: (1) their Sunday morning audience had a basic grasp of biblical teachings and were acquainted with at least forty to fifty Bible stories; (2) church attenders understood and respected the essential boundaries of the Christian worldview, approaching reality with a faith grid into which new ideas could be "deposited" by faithful teachers; (3) those who felt deficient in the above categories could be aroused to pursue further education through self-study or classes.

At the dawn of the twenty-first century the landscape of learning has a very different appearance. I'm no longer fazed when a *majority* of the adults who have gathered for a study struggle to name even one Gospel. I do not assume that those present read anything at all. Recent polls have produced some jaw-dropping insights: the average American invests a mere ten hours annually reading books; college graduates polish off no more than two books per year; nearly one half of the adults in our society are functionally illiterate, incapable of reading or writing beyond an eighth-grade level. Demanding that my elders read a particular book "and please be ready to discuss chapters one through five at the next meeting" is an invitation to frustration. Even the most energized members of our church leave little time in their schedules for reflective reading, and frequently find themselves scrambling to assimilate the basics of scripture.

More disturbingly, what many churchgoers cherish as their personal working knowledge of Christianity is startlingly syncretistic — an amalgam of a few verses here, some New Age notions there, things that Mom once said, and some neat turns of phrase from Hallmark. According to a Barna survey, 81 percent of Americans believe that "God helps those who help themselves" can be found in the Bible. As Will Rogers whimsically said, "It's not what you don't know that will get you in trouble. It's what you know for sure that just ain't so." I've found that every church teaching experience in the last ten years has been improved by assuming that I need to start with Christianity 101. This is not your father's Sunday school.

What's going on here? It's not that aspiring disciples in Indiana are incompetent learners. Something else is happening in contemporary culture. Human beings are drowning in a tidal wave of data. When it comes to business, sports, politics, economics, and religion, there is so much to know that none of us can possibly know even how much we *don't know.* Consider the sheer expansion of human knowledge that has taken place over the last one hundred years. If everything known over the course of human history prior to the year 1900 is considered one unit of human knowledge, then by the year 1950 — just a half century later — what is known had expanded to three units. By the year 1990 our knowledge had expanded to twelve units. And there's no end in sight. This year, at least 65,000 new books will be published. No wonder learners feel discouraged before they even begin.

Even more challenging is the fact that we're living in a time that denies the existence of a universal "truth grid" that might be imposed over the available data so that we might at least make some sense of it. It's controversial even to categorize certain bits of knowledge as important and others as trivial. A *university* was originally designed to be a place where universal truths would make sense of the diversity of all that there is to know. Today's students have little left but the diversity: endless reams of data with no universally acknowledged way to connect the dots.

An acquaintance of mine who lives in the Midwest recently took a walk in the woods. It wasn't long before he realized that he had no idea where he was, nor even what direction he was walking. What came to mind were the wise words of his father, spoken years earlier: "When lost in the woods, son, you can always find north by looking at a tree. The moss always grows on the north side." My friend approached a large tree. To his dismay he discovered that there was moss growing all the way around. "Oh my gosh!" he said. "I'm at the South Pole!"

In today's world, the old markers are failing us. People seeking spiritual truth are lost in an endless forest of data. Is one direction better than another? The problem is that there are too many variables to assess and too many things to know. We suspect that only a few things are worth knowing. But which things? Who will we trust to wade through the oceans of information to tell us what we really need to know?

The hallmark of the Church of the Spirit will be its ability to effectively communicate to its adherents, "This is a place you can trust in your search for what is true. Truth is valued and embraced here." We make no apologies for our counter-cultural conviction that moral and theological imperatives may be discovered and lived out in the smoke and fire of everyday living. We are followers of One who said, "I am the way, the truth, and the life." Our mission is to bring as many individuals as possible to full maturity in Christ, a goal that will be realized only as we seriously embrace our responsibility to teach a new generation the values and truths of Christianity.

At any given time our adult study menu features multiple learning tracks. We sustain at least two or three entry-level study experiences for adults throughout the year. Others are eager to plunge into an intense consideration of theological issues, a particular spiritual discipline, world mission endeavors, a book of the Bible, or historic devotional literature. Members are recurrently called back to exemplify the six marks of the disciple and are reminded that God's mandate is to love God with all our hearts, *minds,* souls, and strength.

Learning traditionally takes place in classrooms. That's a teacher's perspective. The reality is that comparatively few of our youth and adults make the special commitment to attach themselves to a formal class. One study indicates that whereas American church members in the 1950s freed up an average of four "time units" for spiritual activities over the course of a week, today's congregation can expect to see their active members just twice every seven days. We have communicated to new members, "Come to worship and join a small group." Small groups are fast becoming the loci of learning and disciple-making at Zionsville. The teaching is accomplished by six to twelve individuals who communally assume the responsibility to challenge and encourage each other to deeper growth in Christ.

If the one-directional teaching (presenter to students) of the classroom is least transforming, and the learning available through a mini-community of disciples is richer by far, the highest experience of growth and change occurs through a combination of hearing, deciding, and doing. One such learning event took place in our church on a Sunday just prior to Thanksgiving.

The morning message spoke to the need for our members to accept the responsibility for distributing our annual missions budget. That made some eyebrows go up. Each worshiper received a ten-dollar bill in a white envelope. I said, "You're holding God's money in your hand. That's a gift that somebody else gave to God's work. Our invitation this morning is that you be the person to finish the job. Please take your ten dollars and either give it to someone in need or make sure that it helps meet a need in the name of Jesus Christ.

"Where will you find someone in need? Anywhere and everywhere! When you think about it, it's odd that we should assume that just the few people on the Mission Commission of this church would be able to find needy people. You already know people that none of us will ever meet. Please take this small portion and help transform that part of the world where God has planted you. Perhaps you'll want to pool your ten dollars with the money that fellow small group members received, or with family members.

"It's up to you. Be creative. Be prayerful. God will show you what to do. Above all, have fun! Giving with no strings attached accomplishes a work in our hearts that can come about through no other means."

Two weeks later we asked people to let us know what decisions they had made. The results were astonishing. Gifts were made to at least seven foreign countries, and to innumerable local mission agencies. Although there was no express intention to use the ten-dollar bills as "seed money," many families matched or multiplied their gifts in creative ways. Some raised $100 in matching funds from coworkers. One man framed his bill as a permanent reminder to be generous, then wrote a check for $500 to a church ministry.

A family with young children made their ten-dollar bill into a Christmas ornament and pledged to give away at least ten dollars to someone in need every December. Another family pooled their bills to buy a hundred carnations, then passed them out in a nursing home. A woman bought a warm flannel shirt for an elderly man she fondly remembered from her childhood in New England. Several families joined to buy twelve bags of groceries for some friends overburdened by hospital bills.

The most exciting happening was the degree to which families were compelled to talk about the meaning of sharing God's wealth, and then to wrestle to make prayerful decisions. One woman said, "I spent the ten dollars in my mind at least ten times, and I pray the Lord will move me to give another $90 away!" Another spoke for many by saying, "It was a great privilege but a heavy responsibility."

A privilege, a responsibility . . . and a learning experience that taught more about the dynamics of reaching out to others than a hundred sermons on stewardship. A congregation that combines a zeal for truth, a passion to meet needs, and a commitment to let young disciples learn by doing will be effective in the hands of the Spirit indeed.

QUESTIONS FOR REFLECTION AND DISCUSSION

1. What strikes you most deeply about the teaching ministry of Jesus?
2. What are the roles of the teacher in teaching?
3. How do you choose, equip, and empower teachers? What are their goals?
4. What does Pastor McDonald's characterization of the younger generation today call for in our content and style of teaching?
5. How was the distribution of $10 to each member of his congregation an act of teaching as well as mission?

CHAPTER TEN

A Final Word on
How to Use This Book

IMAGINING A Church in the Spirit suggests more than a book title — it is an urgent task for most mainline congregations, both traditional and new start-up churches. We do not believe the ideas proposed in this book will or should be uncritically embraced, but we hope they will be taken seriously.

The foundational aspect of the Church in Jesus Christ and the various expressions he takes in communal form deserve serious and sustained reflection. As pastors, lay leaders, and congregations engage in this task, they will likely pass through different stages. Included in those stages will be entertaining the idea of change, negotiating the exact nature of the changes, training leadership for a Church in the Spirit, experimenting with new forms, adopting these forms and procedures, and maturing in these new options for faithfulness.

Crucial to initiating this process will be the decision to explore the nature of your particular congregation and the options available to it. Nothing happens until you begin the process. Develop a plan and begin to act. Beginning to look at your present church situation in light of the New Testament and the early church commits you to no changes, only to looking and gathering data.

The purpose of this book has been to provide a tool for examining the church's foundation and crucial aspects of its life. You may begin the process by reading this book, by sharing it with other concerned persons, or by adopting it as a study book for officers, Sunday school classes, or adult learning groups. A look at the stages of change may prove reassuring.

Entertaining the Idea

From the opening lines of this book onward we have suggested a variety of reasons why the church at the dawn of the twenty-first century needs to face particular changes. We have set forth a number of ideas to support this point of view. Something has gone wrong with the old model of being and doing church; it is not working for the mainline denominations anymore. Membership decline, loss of political and social influence, and increasing irrelevance in the society mark some of the reasons for change.

A new generation of persons has arisen in North America with very little knowledge of Christian faith. They do not know the words, the scriptures, nor the aims of the churches, and thus find themselves very much on the outside. Reared on television images and values, they possess the attention span of a ten-year-old and they have difficulty appreciating our present modes of worship and music.

These two realities, decline and irrelevance, push numerous mainline congregations further toward death. Granted, not all congregations find their substance in the culture and no congregation is completely dominated by it, but a fading culture does not offer the life of the Spirit. Congregations today need a fresh encounter with Jesus Christ and a renewal of their faith and vision.

But we have further emphasized that the Lord of the church, the present and living Christ, offers himself again as the foundation of the church. He is present to change our lives and our ways of looking at our congregation and mission. He urgently calls us to look to him for life and guidance.

We believe that if your congregation began to look at its life in light of the New Testament, it would discover shocking contrasts. But this shock will be accompanied by the presence of Christ to guide you in revisioning the church.

In laying out the emphases of this book we have tried to choose those seminal aspects of the church's life that need our attention. We offered questions for reflection and discussion in an effort to help a large number of persons in congregations deal with the challenges before us.

Negotiating the Changes

Unambiguously, we have claimed that the church of today needs to change, that it must change for survival if for no other reason. No doubt this challenge evokes enormous fear in the hearts of many who have delighted in the church as it presently exists. Calling for change threatens their source of comfort and cherished memories, and wise leaders will approach it with sensitivity and care. Some may fear new forms of the church, but probably more fear the loss of those experiences and memories that have shaped their lives. In light of these concerns, churches must take the best of the past into the new order for the future. A group of renewalists must not dash off into the future and leave traditionalists in the dust.

The manner in which we have been doing church for decades has not been entirely bad; if it were, the church would not have lasted this long. The cultural church has taught the scripture, observed the liturgy, baptized, married, and cared for people. Who can fault that? Today we are facing a different world with different kinds of people the old forms seem to exclude from our ministry.

Between the church of the past and the church that is being born, we need to negotiate changes at a moderate pace. Even a necessary change can be made so quickly it destroys confidence and heightens barriers to further change. Pace your change at a rate members of the church can appropriate.

Also, beware of the pitfalls of pride, seizing control, and plain stubbornness. When some persons get a new idea and begin to initiate it in the church, they get so full of themselves they turn everyone against them and the proposed changes. Another type of personality decides what the church needs and then seeks to control the process and all the decisions. You will discover another sore spot when you begin negotiating transitions. On both sides of the negotiation you will find sheer stubbornness — one person will be for change and another against it, no matter what it costs.

Training Leadership

The vision set forth in this book cannot be achieved without trained leadership. For decades we have assumed that if a person teaches in the public school or manages a growing business, this same person will make a good teacher in the church school and a dynamic officer in the church. Unfortunately, this illusion still dominates our selection of leadership in congregations. If the church is a spiritual organism, the body of Christ, it requires spiritual leaders.

Those issues with which we have dealt provide an outline of a leadership development course. Leaders in the church begin with a commitment to and love for Christ. New leaders for the Church in the Spirit require skills in evoking community and mending it; they need to learn to pray for the church and trust Christ; they must develop skills in discernment so they will recognize Christ who leads them; they should be persons who believe in and work for the inclusive church; and, they will study to know the faith so that they can teach it to others.

As you seek to become a Church in the Spirit, you will want to plan for the development of mature leaders. Everything seems to depend on the number, quality, and dedication of the leadership. Count on training to be a continuous task.

Experimenting with New Forms

No congregation will initiate a dozen changes at one time, nor should it. As we have pointed out, effective change needs to be paced. The best way to introduce change will be through experiments. Several reasons commend the posture of experimentation as an avenue to change. For one thing, experimentation has a temporary feeling about it. Persons who normally would resist permanent changes will go along with an experiment to see how it works. They assume, and rightly so, that if the experiment doesn't work, the church will go back to its old way.

Experimentation creates security in dealing with new ideas. Someone who cannot buy into a massive change in the worship service, for example, can commit to six weeks of having praise songs as part of the liturgy. So an experiment helps provide safe steps for the timid and fearful. If the test proves beneficial, those who might have been stubborn resisters become strong supporters.

Experimentation also gives a congregation, or a committee of the congregation, permission to fail. Since none of us knows what the church of the twenty-first century should look like, or how it should function, we must test a variety of new forms in diverse settings to discover them. In addition to finding the ways for mainline churches to engage our present context, we will also find ways not to engage it. This means that some experiments will not work. A failed experiment is not a failure if you learn from it.

Our outline sets forth the areas of visioning and experimentation: building community, prayer, initiation, discernment of mission, inclusiveness, and teaching. Each of these has roots in Christ's person and ministry and provides an essential aspect of his body, the church. Explore this essential nature as it manifests itself in Christ; compare and contrast it with your practices, and imagine how it may more faithfully express him to the world today.

Adopting and Implementing

Experimentation leads to new discoveries; when you have discovered a more effective way of being the church, adopt it and implement it. Think about discernment of mission, as an example. We suspect this move will be more difficult for many congregations because of our customary way of "running" the church. Without discounting good management procedures that call for personal and fiscal accountability, we do not believe this secular model offers the best approach for the church. Because this form of leadership has been so deeply ingrained in our thinking, it will likely meet with serious resistance.

When you ask persons to base their plan of ministry on discernment of the will of God, it will immediately raise a number of questions. Does God know about this congregation? Does God care what and how we do our ministry? Can God make known to us what we are to do? Will God do this? All these questions deserve sensitive consideration. Yet, these questions may be an effort to protect the cultural church from coming face to face with God.

Planning a year's work in the traditional way does not force leaders to deal with God. Discernment does. When you ask God, "What do you wish us to do at this time in this place?" you must be prepared for the answer. Frankly, experience has demonstrated to us that people are actually afraid to transact with God in this manner. Our reluctance underscores our need for maturity and training in our relation with God.

When determining your mission and the way you will approach it, we encourage you to bring your request before God. Spend time as officials and committees praying about the needs, resources, and ways to respond. Sit together in silence. Notice what comes to you. Share your insights and let them meld together. Assume for the moment that maybe God does speak to the church in this way.

When you have discerned what you believe to be the will of God, present it to the people. Ask them to pray with you about the discernment. Do they also sense the call of God in what you place before them? If they concur in the plan you have discerned, adopt it and put it into motion.

How can anyone argue with turning to God for guidance? How can anyone speak of prayer as a cop-out? Is it a bad thing if the people of God actually turn to God for guidance and confirmation of the divine will?

We believe that every change suggested in the program for the Church in the Spirit should be addressed in the manner we outlined with respect to discernment of ministry. Prayer, listening, research, study, sharing, and waiting before God suggest the kinds of actions that will be helpful for the entire process.

Maturing in the Process

Once a congregation has begun adopting and implementing changes in its life and ministry, the long road to maturity has been entered but not traversed. Somewhere in your future, say in a year or two when changes have begun to take shape, remember to be grateful. Offer thanks to God for new ideas, new experiments, and new forms that have been put in place and begun to make you a different church. Thankfulness will keep you mindful both of God and the changes.

The congregation that has begun to put new forms in place cannot rest on its achievements. New forms quickly become sacred and traditional. With the pace of change that will certainly mark the future, the church cannot stop changing. Staying alert to changes in the culture and new developments in the community of faith should prod you toward continuous adaptation.

As you process the ideas we have discussed in this book and begin to shift your ways of ministry, a new culture will begin to form in your congregation. We don't know what to call it; perhaps it is the community of the future. The issues we have raised will make a difference in the communal life of the congregation; it will be more open, gracious, and inclusive of differences, and it will require a serious commitment for admission. Decisions will be made in new ways. Worship will have a deeper sense of the presence of God — wonder and awe will occur more often.

The leadership of your church will also be different. Beginning with the minister, the membership will sense a new intensity, a deeper awareness of the Spirit, and a compelling challenge from both his or her lips and life. Officers will no longer veer away from speaking about the faith, praying with fellow members, or sharing in ministry to the poor. You will begin to notice that members of the congregation more frequently feel a call to serve in Christ's name. They will make themselves available more readily or discern ministries for themselves.

As these changes begin to occur in your congregation, the word will flow out of your meetings to the surrounding community; new persons will show up for worship or to participate in the special ministries you offer. These changes will clearly mark you as a Church in the

Spirit. When these signs appear in your congregation, your task of imagining the church has not been completed but it has made marked progress.

Each year of the new millennium, the Church in the Spirit will meet in hope. Celebration will characterize its gatherings, and year by year the congregation will change in response to the Spirit's guidance in an ever-changing world. Christ will be honored! God will be glorified! And, the kingdom will be coming — day by day by day!

May God be with you on this journey!

Index of Subjects

Index of Scripture References

Matthew

5:1-16	132
7:22-23	69
14:23-32	63
28:20	27

Mark

1:14-20	42
1:22-27	43
1:29-22	132
4:3-11	42
6:7-13	44
6:31	69

Luke

4:1-2	62
6:12-13	63

9:28-32	64
11:1-4	64
22:1-13	134

John

1:29-31	41
1:38-41	42
14:18-20	9
15:16	90
16:12-15	9

Acts

1:8	27
2:41-47	26
2:44	33

I Corinthians

3:10-15	8
3:16-17	11
12:12-27	23
12:17-18	114-15
12:27	11, 12, 20
14:23-26	32

Galatians

3:26-29	107

Ephesians

4:8-13	138
5:25-27	14

I Peter

2:10	11